AF443807

The Drunken Hamster Electric Boogaloo

Tony Marshall

The Drunken Hamster Electric Boogaloo

2005

2020 15th Anniversary Reprint Edition

To Amee'

For laughing at all my stupid jokes, tolerating my
silly writing habit, and most of all, being the love and
inspiration of my life.

Acknowledgements

This book wouldn't have existed without my parents, Jerry and Tam Marshall. Thank you for the lifelong encouragement that I could do anything if I keep God first, as well as that whole "giving birth to me" thing. And, Daddy, thanks for buying those 25¢ SuperFlyer books from me when I was younger.

Also, although you can't read this yet, thank you Wilson and Jacob, my two little monkeys, and the yet unnamed monkey #3 for always putting a smile on my face and being the greatest blessing my life has ever had.

Next to last but definitely not least, thank you to the Tony Marshall Fan Club for your constant support for now over three years! You guys and gals are the best, and I want you to know that I appreciate each and every one of you, even the jerks that wouldn't shut their mouths on TTMFC forums.

And of course, the ultimate thanks goes to my Lord and Savior Jesus Christ, who is worthy of all our highest praise.

Table of Contents

Introduction

You're holding in your hands the greatest book ever written. Well, maybe not the greatest; that would be the Bible. Actually, it's probably not number two, three, or four either, as I'm kinda partial to a few other books that would probably fall into those slots. Truth be known, I'd say it's number 12,357, tops. So maybe that first sentence should have read: You're holding in your hands the greatest book *I've* ever written.

I should clarify something before continuing. You see, I'm not much of a writer; in fact, if you were to classify me as anything I'd say you'd pretty much call me a world-class doofus.

I'm telling you this because I figure it's only fair to warn you upfront of what you're getting into by reading this book.

I never paid much attention in English class except when we read something that I considered funny, and even then I mostly just read the Cliffs Notes. Needless to say, the grammar stuff went in one ear and out the other too. Sometimes it didn't even go in; it just kinda bounced off a lobe. Plus I don't use Q-Tips according to the instructions on the box and I cram them way down in my ears, probably packing lots of cotton in there in the process. I even debated typing this book in Microsoft Notepad instead of Microsoft Word because I was tired of Word drawing green lines under all my sentences.

Yet somehow despite my lack of attention span in school, I developed the desire to write a book. That's a pretty lofty goal for someone with a complete lack of talent and the attention span of a two-year-old child. But luckily, stubbornness and the ability to be totally oblivious to what people think of me are two of my talents, so I'm writing a book despite my shortcomings.

About twenty years and hundreds of crumpled balls of paper later, my attempts at writing a "properly written" or "grammatically correct" or even "somewhat interesting" book have fallen dreadfully short of hitting the mark, so I'm reduced to my last resort: writing the same way I talk and think. Those of you that know me personally are probably shuddering right now. Those of you that don't know me will probably shudder at the thought of meeting me by the end of this book.

The "way I talk and think" can basically be described in the very least as crude. When I say crude, I don't mean it in a vulgar way, I mean crude in an unrefined Jeff Foxworthy redneck definition way: a glorious lack of sophistication.

One of the main problems with writing the way I talk and think is that, like writing, I don't talk and think with "proper technique."

My brain is pretty much a jumbled up mess of short snippets of unrelated thoughts, random pictures, long laundry lists of rankings and to-do lists, long winded ramblings from many many personalities (including an orangutan), lots of gee-whiz trivia-type knowledge, and that stupid "Song That Doesn't End" playing over and over again. Oh yeah, and video game cheat codes. So, that's pretty much what you're getting into when you read this book: a jumbled up mess of short snippets of unrelated thoughts, random pictures, long laundry lists of rankings and to-do lists, long winded ramblings from many many personalities (possibly including an orangutan), lots of gee-whiz trivia-type knowledge, sans the "Song That Doesn't End" due to the lack of multimedia capabilities. I might even throw in a cheat code or two (up, up, down, down, left, right, left, right, B, A).

Hopefully if you reach the end of this book, you'll finally be able to answer one of the top three questions that most of my friends ask me: "What is going on in your head?" (the other two questions being "When did you start losing your hair?" and "You're not really going to do that, are you?").

To make the overall experience more bearable for you, I'll make you the following promises:

> 1.)　**I'll try my best to avoid using really big words**, which is a good idea since I don't really know many in the first place. I do, however, reserve the right to use as many imaginary really big words as I want, because they're easier to use than words that I actually have to research. And I'm also going to use the word "discombobulated" a fair amount too, but that's just because it's a fun word.
>
> 2.)　**No harsh language**, unless you consider words like "poot," "tinkle," "squishy," and in extreme circumstances, "Hillary Clinton," harsh.
>
> 3.)　**I'll write at least one third of this book while wearing nothing but my underwear**, so you can feel more comfortable about the way you'll be reading most of this book: either in your underwear or while sitting on the toilet. I originally was going to promise I would be in my underoos for at least one *half* of the book, but then I realized I might write

some of it while at my workplace and it would be awkward for others around me (or awkward for me if they don't seem to mind).

4.)   **If you feel like skipping around while reading, go for it.** As I said before, my thoughts are pretty random so you will probably be okay skipping around. I would recommend reading Chapter Tree before moving on past it, as I introduce an important character, SuperFlyer, in that chapter. If you skip Chapter Tree, you may end up discombobulated.

5.)   **No mention of politics.** Talking about politics drives my wife crazy and I can understand why. When you hear about all the dishonest things these politicians do and how much of our tax dollars they spend doing it, you have tendency to get angry. This one time I read about a politician who got a tank, a goat, and a wheel of Gouda cheese and — sorry, there I go talking about politics. Okay, so no more politics from this point on.

6.)   **This will be a short book.** This one is easy to prove, since you can just flip to the last page and see how many pages there are. This promise is easy to for me to accomplish too, since, as I said before, I'm not much of a writer and I would have great difficulty filling up more than a hundred pages or so unless there were lots of drawings. Drawings…hmmm… Anyhow, I'm not so concerned with filling up a lot of pages. I'm not going to do like I used to do when I was in grade school and needed to fill up a bunch of pages on a writing assignment, and I would just write something like: "The man was tall. He was also very

very very very very very very very very
very very very very very very very very
very very very very very very very very
very very very very very very very very
very very very very very very very very
very very very very very very very very
very very very very very very very very
very very very very very very very very
very very very very very very very very
very very very very very very very very
very very very very very very very very
very very very very very very very very
very very very very very very very very
very very very very very very very very
very very very very very very very very
very very very very very very very very
very very very very very very very very
very very very very very very very very
very very very very very very very very
very very very very very very very very
very very very very very very very very
very very very very very very very very
very very very very very very very very
very very very very very very very very
very very very very very very very very
very very very very very very very very
very very very very very very very very
very very very very very very very very
very very very very very very very very
very very very very very very very very

very very very very very very very very
very very very very very very very very
very very very very very very very very
very very very very very very very very
very very very very very very very very
very very very very very very very very
very very very very very very very very
very very very very very very very very
very very very very very very very very
very very very very very very very very
very very very very very very very very
very very very very very very very very
very very very very very very very very
very very very very very very very very
very very very very very very very very
very very very very very very very very
very very very very very very very very
very very very very very very very very
very very very very very very very very
very very very very very very very very
very very very very very very very very
very very very very very very very mean
and ugly too." I'm not gonna do that.

Well, I guess that's about it. I've laid
down the groundwork for my writing style, so
consider yourself warned. If you continue on
after this point, you have no excuses for being
upset. You'd be like the person that tries suing

the tobacco company claiming that they didn't know that smoking causes cancer.

That being said, I hope you enjoy this book. If you actually *purchased* this book, thank you from the bottom of my heart. I'm going to buy a cup of coffee from Starbucks in your honor with the money I made off the sale (a small cup). If by some miracle you think I did a good job at writing this book, feel free to drop me a line at my website, www.tonymarshall.net and let me know.

If you think I did a bad job, still let me know, because I'd like to chuckle at how I wasted an hour or so of your time (if you could tell me the exact amount of time I would appreciate that too).

Happy reading, God bless, and I hope you don't get too discombobulated.

Chapter Juan

Bed time. Many books start off at the beginning of the day, so I thought I'd be different. Besides, bedtime is when all the hamsters in my head get off their respective wheels and start partying. The resulting chaos is something to behold. Some people like to call this chaos "dreaming." I call it what it really is: the drunken hamster electric boogaloo.

Lately I've been fascinated with the drunken hamster electric boogaloo, or dreaming, as I will refer to it now for those of you that are easily confused. There seems to be a small pocket of the scientific community that has devoted itself to studying the drunken—er, dreaming. Scientists in this community have determined that dreaming happens during an increased period of electrical brain activity (hmmm...electric boogaloo, anyone?) that is accompanied by a crazed jumping around of the eyes, also known as Rapid Eye Movement or REM, not to be confused with the popular 90's rock group.

These scientists, who have forsaken normal food and now rely on a steady diet of intravenously fed coffee, believe that with proper technique a person can achieve lucid dreaming—or the ability to be aware that he or she is dreaming and actually control it. They believe that if a person is somehow given a "dream signal," or something that lets them know that they're dreaming while not waking them up, they could achieve this lucid dreaming. Typically, this is achieved by monitoring the REM cycles of a sleeper, and then shining bright red lights into the sleeper's eyes when they start doing the eyeball tango. Apparently your brain is supposed to notice the lights, and with proper training, say "hey, we're dreaming! Yay! No consequences to our actions!" And then you go nuts and do whatever you want in your dreams.

Ignoring the horrible social ramifications that could occur from getting people used to the idea that they can do anything they want, and the fact that your brain shuts off your optic nerves when you go to sleep and you can't see lights when you're asleep, I've decided to experiment. Apparently you can purchase a "dream machine" from uppity technology companies that have nothing better to sell than fantastic new gadgets that don't work. These machines are basically sleeping masks with Christmas lights taped on the inside of them that are designed to start blinking after a certain time delay. Seeing as I don't want to spend $500 on such a device, and that I don't own a sleeping mask (and have no desire to own one) with which to make my own version of the machine, I've decided to go low-tech and get my wife to shine a flashlight in my face when she sees that my eyes are shuffling about. The conversation goes something like this:

"Hey, Amee', do me a favor…"

"What is it this time?"

"Point this Mag-Lite at my face and turn it on when I go to sleep and you see my eyes start darting around."

Amee' sighs loudly.

"Aw, come on, just do it!"

"What do I get in return?"

"You get the satisfaction of helping me make a huge scientific breakthrough."

Once again, a loud sigh.

"You're not trying to grow your hair back again, are you? Remember when you got baking soda all over the place and it clogged up the vacuum? We had to borrow Momma's Thermax to get it up."

"No, nothing messy this time, I promise. And I'll give you a back rub. And I'll make you a bacon sandwich."

"Fine. But it better not be one of your one-handed-fall-asleep-after-two-minutes back rubs."

"Deal."

So I handed her the flashlight and it was off to la-la land…or so I thought.

Have you ever tried to make yourself go to sleep? Remember trying to fall asleep as a kid the night before Christmas? This task ranks right up there with being a one-legged man trying to learn how to rollerblade. It's not impossible, just extremely difficult.

After about fifteen minutes of staring at the back of my eyelids, I determined that I needed a new strategy if I was to fall asleep anytime soon. I considered popping a few Tylenol PM to help me out, but then I felt that would skew the results of my experiment (by the way, some of you might think that it's a bad idea to take Tylenol PM when you just need to go to sleep but don't have a headache, but I submit that when you're the father of two toddlers you *always* have a headache). The next idea was to drink some sort of relaxing herbal tea, but there's that whole *"you have to get up and make it"* thing. The idea of counting sheep came next, but

26

somehow while I was lost in the thought of whether or not counting only white sheep was somehow racist, all of my hamsters punched their respective time clocks and jumped off their wheels. I was asleep.

It was time to get down to business. Of course, I didn't realize this, since no one had yet shined a light in my face. I was actually in that brain shut down phase, kinda like older Windows 98 computers that had that screen that said "It is now safe to turn off your computer."

I've read that dreaming is supposedly your brain's way of dealing with and processing all the information that has been pumped into it during the day, so one might argue that during this shutdown phase my brain was starting to sort through the day's events. I know this is not true because I can hear all the rodents in my head donning their baggy pants and practicing their Whodini and MC Hammer lyrics. I can't really tell you *exactly* what goes on during this sleep phase since the experiment ultimately turned out to be a failure (don't act surprised, if it worked don't you think I'd be dreaming right now instead of clacking away on a keyboard?), but I can tell you what ended up waking me up: the Mag-Lite.

Oh, I don't mean the Mag-Lite woke me up because it was shining so brightly in my eyes. The reason I woke up was because my violent little redheaded son decided to whack me upside the head with it. In case you don't know what a Mag-lite is, it's a heavy metal flashlight that is available in a variety of sizes. And this Mag-Lite was of the two-inch thick foot-long variety.

Whoever said that redheads are mean and/or hot-tempered couldn't have been more right. My little two-year old redheaded fatboy, Jacob, is a little spitfire. He actually balances his temper quite well and has a very sweet and polite side and he's generally very good natured, but every now and then something clicks in his brain and he decides that the world is a huge whack-a-mole game and he has the only mallet. And it's a huge mallet.

Apparently he had woken in the middle of the night and crawled into our bed. Upon doing so, he found the bright blue Mag-Lite that Amee' had abandoned in order to get some sleep of her own. And from what I've been able to piece together in the blurry aftermath, a shiny bald head is far too tempting of a target for a two-year old with a bludgeoning tool to pass up. I guess I should be thankful that he didn't find a sharpie to write all over my face with as well.

I guess I should admire my son's work ethic. I mean, beating the mess out of me is apparently part of his job, and he was doing it during what should've been his off hours. You don't see that very much in America these days.

28

Most of us are so spoiled by technology that we don't even remember what real work is.

In the past, the drive behind developing technology was the desire to get work done more efficiently.

Technically, this is still true today; however, the focus is different, as in the past people generally wanted to be more efficient so they could do more work in a given period of time (as in, "hey, if I can get the wall to this cabin built more quickly, I can help Aunt Suzie churn the butter so we can have some good vittles tonight! Plus we won't die from freezing to death due to the lack of a cabin wall" or "If I just get ten more units manufactured today I can start on Project X and actually take pride in my work"). Today, people want to be more efficient so they can do as little work as possible and spend more time doing absolutely nothing or playing solitaire. Some people are so lazy that they'll go out of their way and work harder at being lazy than they ever would have worked at doing an actual job.

Being lazy doesn't just occur at the workplace. People are lazy in everyday situations as well. Here are some actual products I've seen in stores (okay, Wal-Mart): Gift wrap opener, for getting the gift wrap off of presents (since tearing paper is incredibly difficult and no one likes opening presents).

Electric scissors, which might not be a bad idea for someone who has arthritis or for someone who cuts fabric all day long, except that the front of the box says: "for your everyday cutting needs," since everyday I avoid cutting with scissors since it's such an arduous task. Crustless bread, because you can't take the time to cut the edges off your kid's bread, since bread is one of the hardest substances known to man (okay, I have to admit I actually thought this one was kinda neat...not so much because I thought it was such a time-saver, just mostly because I could envision a loaf of bread running through a machine that looks like one of those log-bark removers, and I always thought that was cool). Coffee filter tongs, because three seconds is way too long to have to fiddle around with getting a single coffee filter separated from the rest of the bunch. I actually have more items for my list, but I'm too lazy to finish writing it.

I guess Agatha Christie put it best when she said, "I don't think necessity is the mother of invention—invention, in my opinion, arises directly from idleness, possibly also from laziness. To save oneself trouble."

Did I mention it's bedtime? It's time to sleep...albeit with a headache.

Chapter Too

I know the cure for cancer. Baking soda. Yep, baking soda. I just have to run a few more experiments before I'm absolutely certain, but I'm about 96.3% sure. I also haven't figured out how exactly you would actually apply the baking soda, whether it would be a topical ointment of sorts or something you ingest. I've pretty much narrowed it down to drinking it mixed with cherry soda or mixing it with guano and rubbing it all over the general area of the cancer (you probably don't want to go into public after doing this one). Eating broccoli in conjunction with one of these methods couldn't hurt either.

If you think I'm way off on this one, think about it for a moment. What can't baking soda do? You can brush and whiten your teeth with it. You can freshen up your fridge and freezer with it. You can sprinkle it in your underwear and get the stank out. You can mix it with vinegar and make a volcano. You can probably use it with some duct tape and make an H-bomb. Heck, I even think there's some sort of baking purpose for it.

Still not convinced? Here is a list of 38 other proven uses for baking soda:

1.)   Fire extinguisher
2.)   Vegetable and fruit cleaner
3.)   Laundry booster
4.)   Cleaner for the terminal posts on automobile batteries
5.)   Hairbrush cleaner
6.)   Coffee Pot cleaner
7.)   Oil absorber
8.)   Silver tarnish remover
9.)   Baked-on food remover
10.)   Chrome polisher
11.)   Smolder preventative for ash trays
12.)   Rain repellant for car windshields (like Rain-X)
13.)   Shower curtain refresher
14.)   Bathwater additive (softens skin)
15.)   Diaper rash treatment
16.)   Insect bite treatment
17.)   Chicken pox and measles treatment
18.)   Mouthwash (when mixed with water)
19.)   Canker sore treatment
20.)   Sunburn treatment (when mixed with water and used as a paste)
21.)   Play clay for kids (when mixed with water and cornstarch)

22.) Play clay for adults (when you're nothing but a big kid)

23.) Chicken feather removal aid (seriously!)

24.) Drain treatment

25.) Digestion aid

26.) Deep splinter remover (soak affected area in a warm water and baking soda solution for 20 minutes a day until the splinter simply pops out)

27.) Dog shampoo

28.) Wallpaper cleaner

29.) Gas stove burner de-clogger

30.) Fever reducer

31.) Paint remover (for dried-on paint on paintbrushes)

32.) Pesticide (roaches dehydrate when they eat it…cool!)

33.) Rabbit repellant

34.) Vaporizer additive (unblocks stuffed nasal passages – you can even make a nasal spray with it)

35.) Eyeglass cleaner

36.) Heartburn remedy

37.) Soil acid tester

38.) Underarm deodorant

See? I'm not so crazy after all. Well, not about the baking soda thing at least. I figure scientists are just guessing when it comes to curing diseases anyhow, and I think the same statement can apply to doctors.

My Dad once went to the doctor for a routine checkup and the doctor had told him that the continual chest pains he was experiencing while taking his daily walk were probably just a result of gas (since when he burped the pain would go away), but *just in case* he should visit a cardiologist.

When he visited the specialist, the cardiologist had determined that he had two blocked arteries, one of them being a major artery and it was around 99% blocked. My Dad had to have an immediate double bypass, and thanks to the Lord, is still with us today. Luckily the cardiologist knew what he was doing, but I'm fairly convinced that if it weren't for God smacking the original doctor upside the head with some common sense, that doctor would have just given my Dad his thirtieth gas pill prescription and sent him on his way.

I also don't like the "I'm smarter than you and you couldn't possibly understand your own medical condition so I'm not going to explain it to you" attitude that the majority of the medical community has. Those of you in the medical community shouldn't get offended by this. First of all, I said *most* of the medical community, not *all*. Secondly, if you do get offended, I'm probably talking about you specifically, so deal with it.

Here's an example of what I'm referring to in reference to this arrogant attitude: My Dad went for yet another routine checkup (he's a Veteran—they have lots of these) and some blood work was done on him. They told my Dad that his blood work had come back "abnormal," with no further explanation but to tell him that they needed to do further blood work *just in case*.

Now, I fully respect covering all bases and am glad that doctors do things *just in case*, as my Dad quite possibly might not be around right now if not for the previous *just in case*, but more and more I'm beginning to realize that *just in case* means "I have no idea what I'm doing so I better try again or pawn this off on someone else" (Once again, this is fine, as I would rather go through twenty tests and determine I'm sick and then get the proper treatment than go through one test and be told I'm fine only to have my chest explode a week later. However, would it kill a doctor to say "Gosh, I really don't know the answer to this problem?").

Anyhow, they did further blood work, handed my Dad a piece of paper with a medical readout, and said the new results were "inconclusive." And that was all. No further explanation. Gee, thanks for the peace of mind. Now we could all sleep better at night.

But, *just in case*, me and my Dad did some detective work and deciphered the "inconclusive" results. We determined that the only items in his blood work that were abnormal (the abnormal items were indicated on the paper they gave us), were direct byproducts of a low-carb diet, which my Dad happened to be on at the time. How did we determine this? We put every one of the items in a search engine on the internet and looked at the results. It was really tough. My index finger was a little sore afterwards. My little brain was pounding and the hamsters in my head were breathing so hard that their eyes were bulging and their hair was falling out. If I had only gone to school for eight years before looking up this information I would have been able to decipher this nigh-unbreakable code more easily, and I would've have seen right away that the answer was that these results were in fact "inconclusive."

Is it too much to ask for the medical school curriculum to include an extra course: common courtesy? Handwriting might be a good course to add too. Nothing beats getting a prescription for birth control pills when you were supposed to get a diarrhea suppository. I've heard that some hospitals are now requiring doctors to take a handwriting course, so at least that's a step in the right direction. But why isn't it a standard in school, before they even step into the hospital? Are bad handwriting and a crass attitude just another way of saying "you're too stupid to comprehend what I'm doing?"

Once again, I'd like to point out that I'm not talking about all doctors. My family and I have had some really good doctors. Doctor Bolton (no relation to Michael, to my understanding, which is admirable), the doctor who delivered our first son, was top-notch. When we had our second child, my job had moved us about ninety miles away from Doctor Bolton's office, and we actually considered driving an hour and a half just to have her deliver him.

I guess what all I'm trying to say is that if we all just started eating more baking soda, soaking in it in our baths, and applying it as a paste to choice areas of our bodies, we can eliminate the majority of the medical community as we will live in near perfect health. It's true, or my name isn't Bocephus McFadelton.

Chapter Tree

Jerry Seinfeld placed a Superman reference (usually a statue or a picture of some sort) in almost every episode of his TV show, *Seinfeld.* I respect this, as I have had a love of superheroes as long as I can remember *[for those of you that know me personally, insert joke about my terrible memory here]*, and Superman was right at the top of the list.

When I was kid my friends and I would argue about superheroes—who was stronger and who could beat up who and such (we agreed that He-Man was probably stronger than Superman, but Superman would win in a fight because he was almost as strong, but he also had the option of burning He-Man, freezing him, or performing a flying jump kick on him. Plus he could melt He-Man's sword). Finally, after months of arguing, I decided to put an end to the arguments by making my own superhero, one who could beat the heck out of any other superhero without question.

I named my creation SuperFlyer. And yes, I spelled it Flyer, not Flier (according to the dictionary, it can actually be spelled both ways, but I didn't know that when I was a kid).

I don't remember exactly how old I was when I made SuperFlyer, but I'm guessing I was around seven years old. That being said, my "creation" consisted of taking Superman and changing his colors from blue and red to a darker navy blue and orange, respectively. Why those two colors? Because they were the longest two crayons in my box that weren't something girlie like pink or magenta (pronounced mag-neta back in those days). Besides the color of his outfit, pretty much the only differences were his name (including his secret identity, Brad McKenzie, which I never seemed to spell the same way twice) and the fact that he could beat up *any* other super hero, if needs be.

I made little books starring SuperFlyer and would "sell" them to my Dad for 25¢. Of course, somehow they kept ending up back in my possession.

The plot would pretty much be the same every time: SuperFlyer flies around, he spots a villain, fights the villain, beats up the villain, and turns back into his "normal person." "Normal person" was the term I used meaning "secret identity."

I got pretty creative when I created the villains. I remember once Super Flyer fought the Croquet Man. He had absolutely nothing to do with croquet, but we had just gotten a new croquet set and I liked the word. Croquet Man

40

had a clam shaped head and claws for hands, so what would you have called him? Clam-crab guy? I don't think so. If my memory serves me correctly, Croquet Man had a sidekick that, appropriately enough, looked exactly like Croquet Man only smaller. I don't think he had a name, though. Maybe it was Mini-Croquet Man.

I recently unearthed one of my SuperFlyer books, entitled *The New SuperFlyer Three*. I have no idea if it was actually the third SuperFlyer book or not. Knowing me, it was probably the fifth one and I just forgot what number I was on when I was naming it.

You're probably incredibly enthralled right now with SuperFlyer, so would you like to read it? No? Well, tough, you're gonna read it anyway. And you're gonna like it too, or my name isn't Seamus McFoofoo.

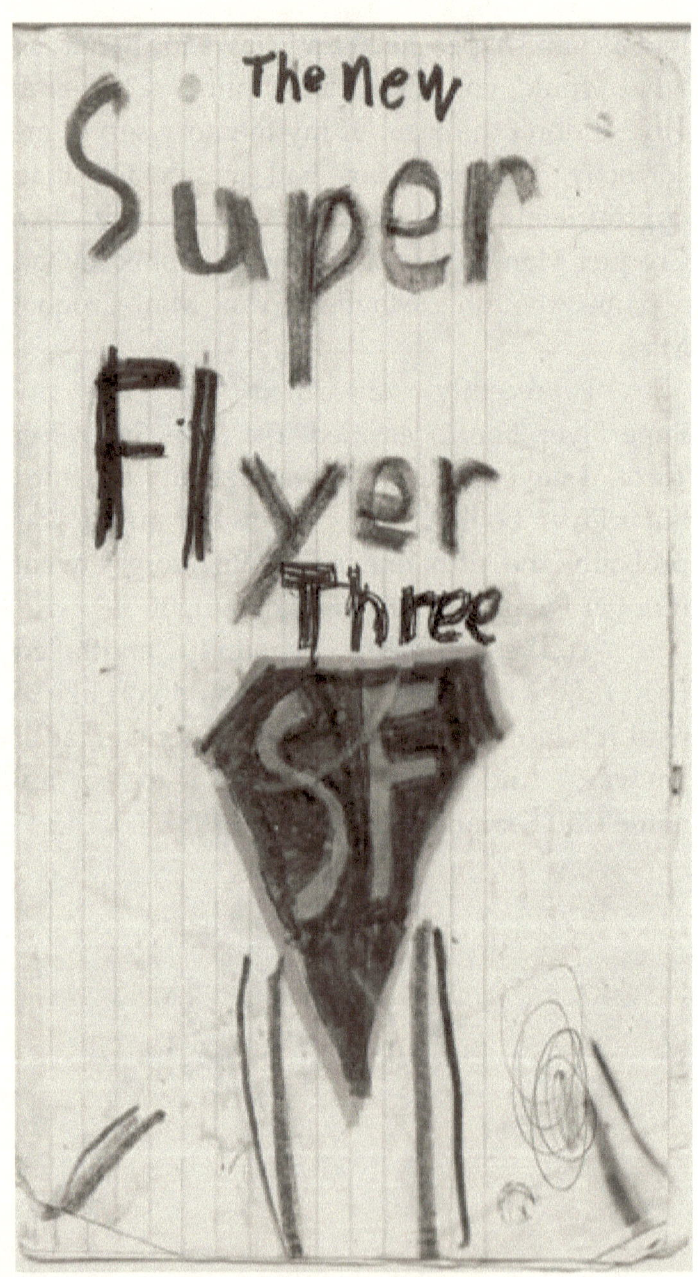

The New Super Flyer Three

Super Flyer could fly.

How could the bad guy get super-flyer.

Super Flyer saw Madness-man.

Super Flyer hit a bem back.

The bad guy flew away.

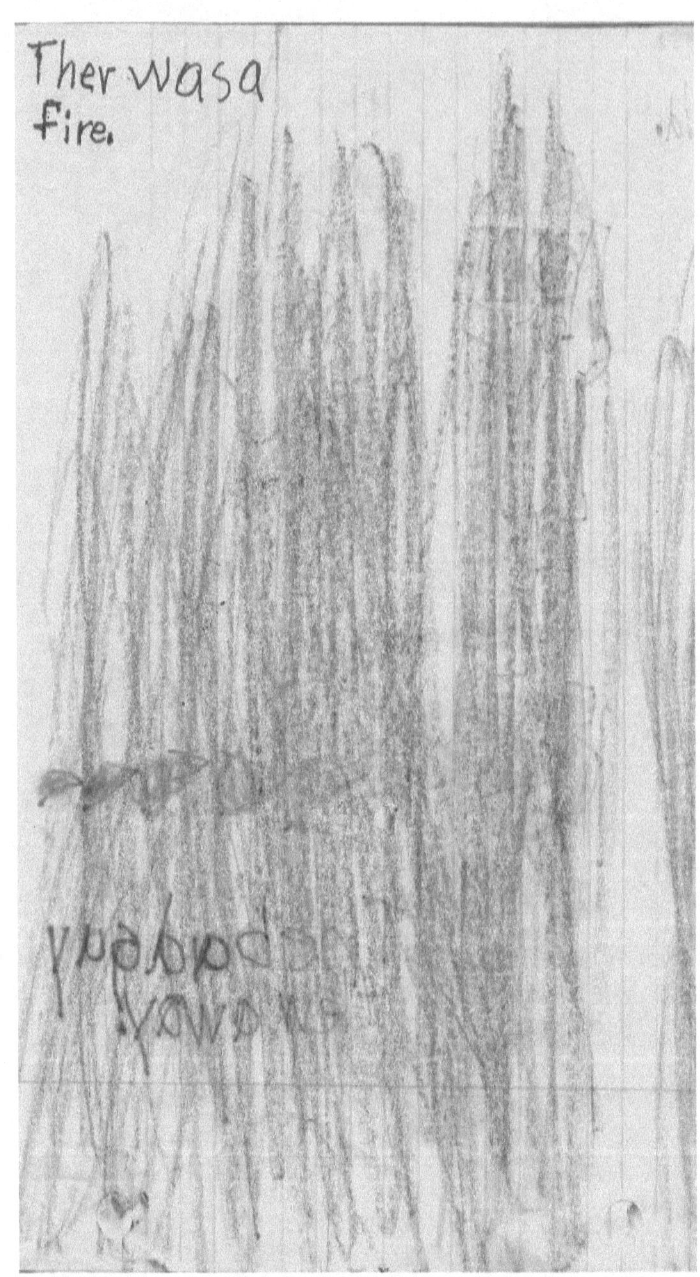

Ther was a fire.

Super Flyer blew it out.

It was cold.

It was cold because Superflyer blew out the fire.

"Oh no"

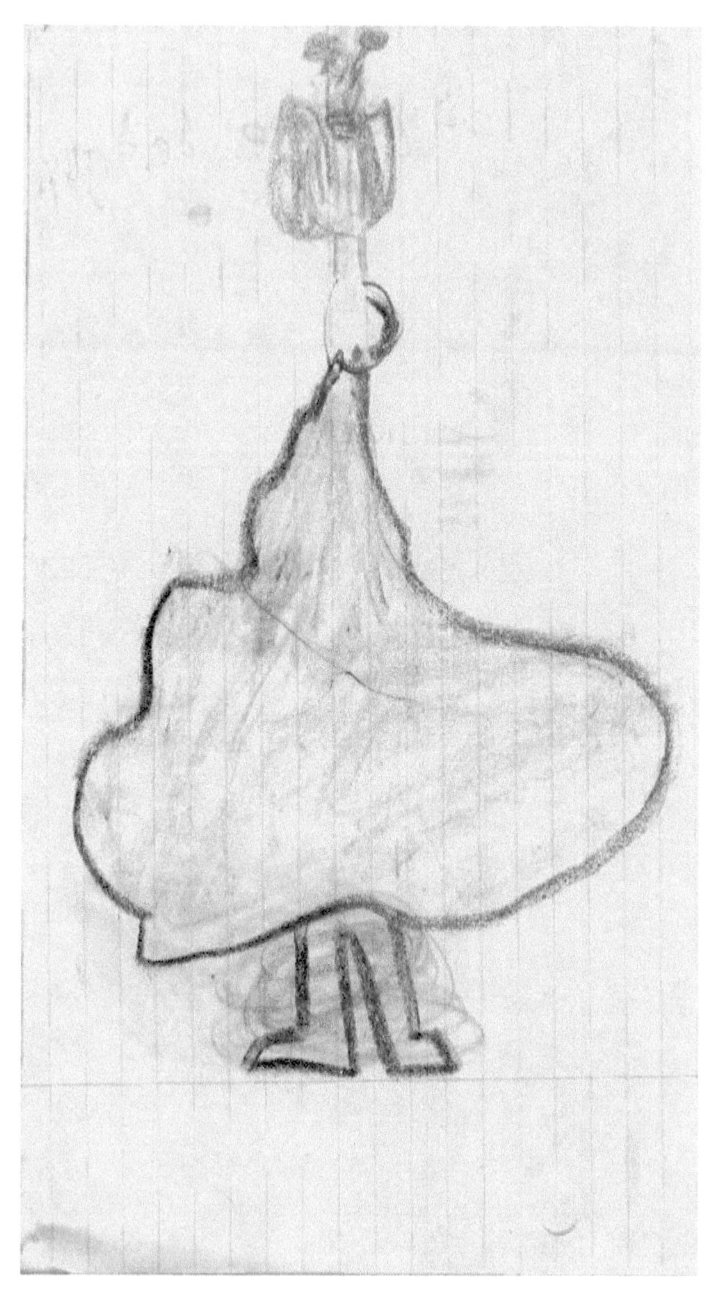

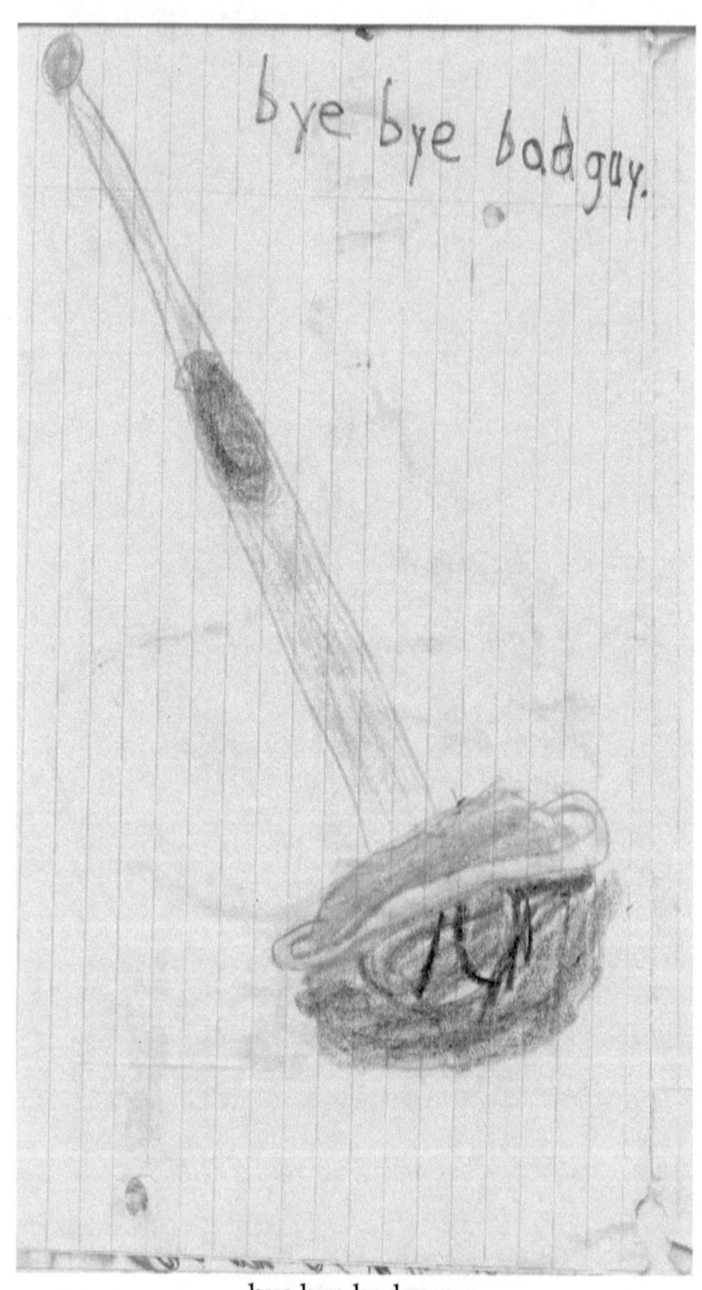

bye bye badguy.

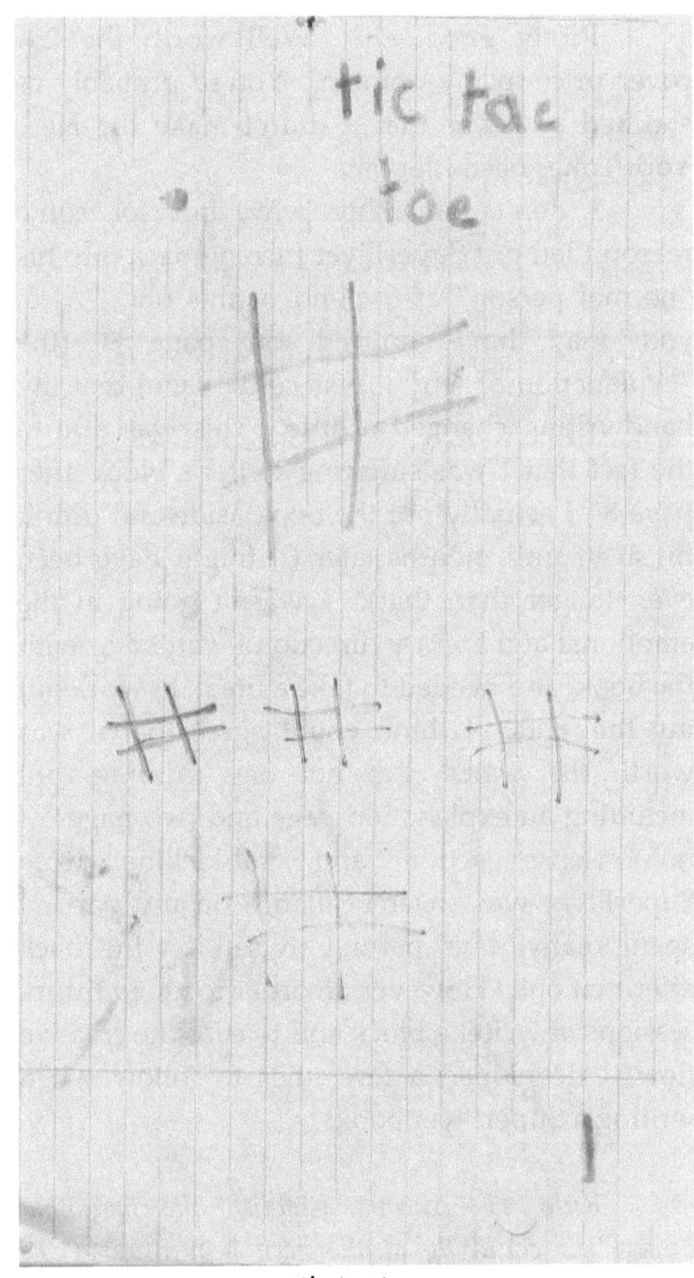

tic tac toe

Pretty good, eh? Well worth the 25¢ cover price in my opinion. You're probably as shocked as I was that it didn't make the New York Times bestseller list.

I don't remember why, but for some reason I left out SuperFlyer turning back into his "normal person" at the end of this one. Also, you may have noticed on page 9 (the "explanation of why it was cold" page) that my handwriting changed a little. This was due to the fact that I was suffering writer's block after page 8. I actually put the book aside and didn't finish it until months later (it might have been even longer than that). I wasn't going in the emotional and literary direction I wanted to with the book, and needed to take a break to work out my thoughts. I think you'll agree that it was worth the wait. I'm not one to brag, but including an explanation page and two pages of no-nonsense action and tail-kicking from SuperFlyer was sheer brilliance on my part. I spent many days patting myself on the back after that one. However, in order to avoid future sessions of writer's block and to ease the creative flow, I developed a few rules to follow when writing a SuperFlyer book:

Rule #1—Always establish the fact that SuperFlyer could fly at the very beginning of the story. You don't want people to be in the middle of the book when SuperFlyer first flies, because they just might not understand what's going on.

*   **Rule #2**—Bad guys can't have normal hands. They either have to be some sort of projectile weapon, animal claw, or nub. A combination of any of these will work as well.*

*   **Rule #3**—As the story nears the end, words are not necessary. They only bog down the plot. An exclamation by the villain indicating the fear of impending doom is acceptable.*

*   **Rule #4**—Always shoot the bad guy into space after you beat him up.*

*   **Rule #5**—A period is the only acceptable punctuation, regardless if you write a statement, question, or exclamation.*

*   **Rule #6**—If you have an extra blank page at the end of the book, go ahead and place some sort of fun activity there for your readers to do to keep them occupied until the next SuperFlyer book comes out.*

It's a no-lose situation if I use these rules. I could even make a book today using these rules and it would turn out as great as the originals. No, really! I know that many times when a remake of a book/movie/TV show is produced they aren't as good as the original, but the 6-step formula is flawless. I'll prove it to you. May I present to you: The New New SuperFlyer Three!

The New New Super Flyer Three

SuperFlyer could fly.

The bad guy wanted to get Super Flyer.

SuperFlyer saw Captain Mung.

Captain Mung shot some mung at Super Flyer.

Super Flyer flew out of the way.

Super Flyer hocked a loogie at Captain Mung to pay
him back for shooting Mung at him.

The bad guy was discombobulated.

Captain Mung flew away. (to take a shower).

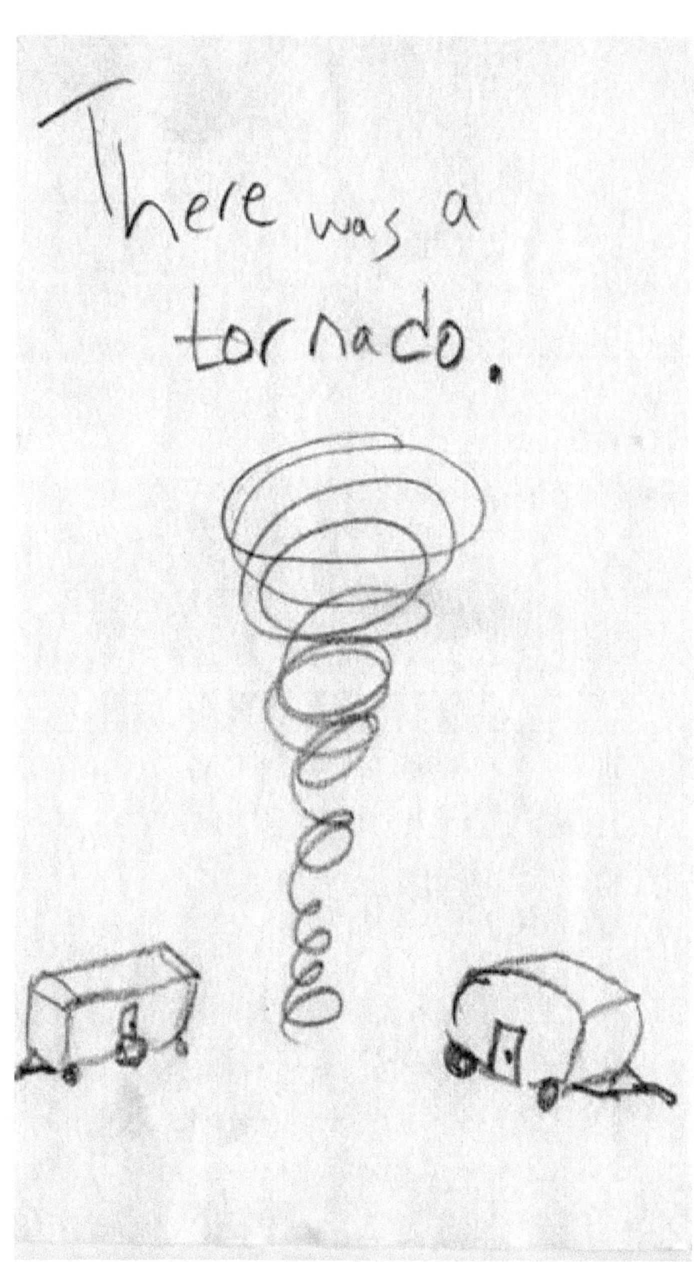

There was a tornado.

Super Flyer blew away the tornado.

It was wet and swampy.

It was wet and swampy because Super Flyer blew away the tornado and had a lot of drool in his mouth. He also had bad funk breath.

"burgerfickle."

Bye bye bad guy.

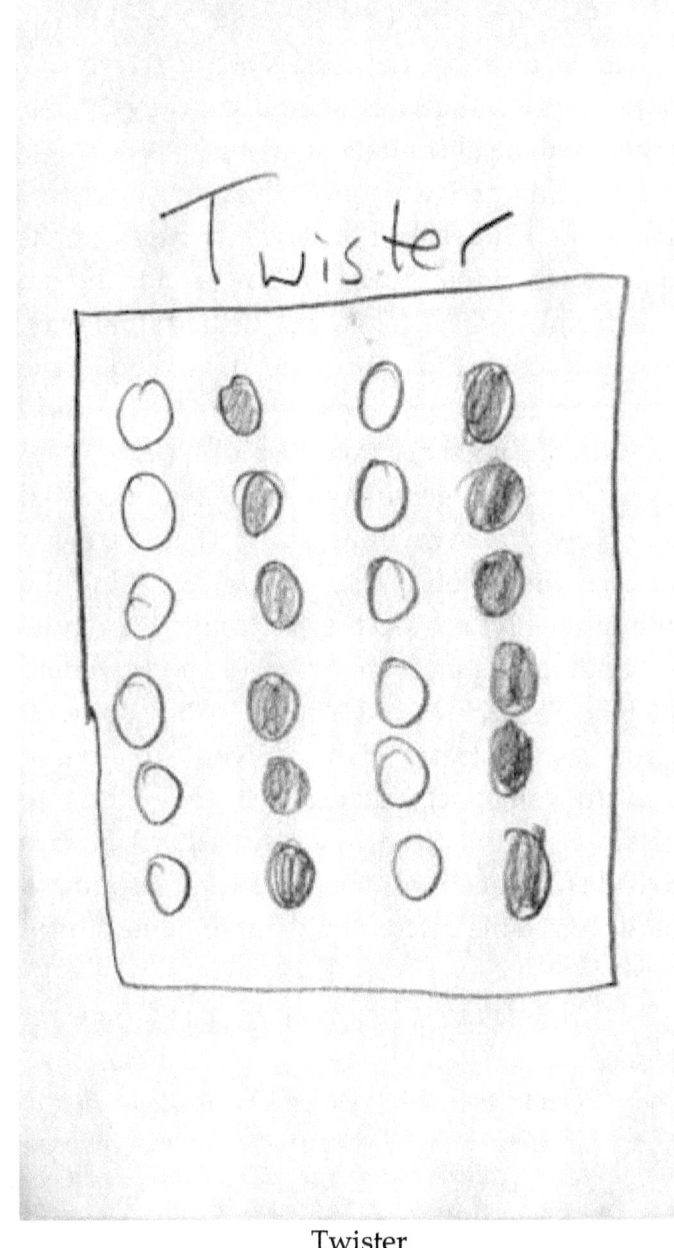

Twister

See? It's a can't-fail formula. I might even make an entire new series of SuperFlyer books. I've got the rules, so you know every one of them will be absolutely amazing.

Seeing as I was only seven or so when I thought up SuperFlyer, I never went as far as thinking up SuperFlyer's origin (as in, did he come from another planet, was he born that way, etc.), but if I did I'm sure it would have something to do with baking soda. That, and either orange soda or Pepto Bismol.

Origins in general have always interested me. How did everything start? I don't mean this in the Biblical sense, as in "In the beginning...", I'm referring to things like "how did languages start?" and "who really invented the wheel?" How did people come up with words like "abstract?" How do you explain that word to someone, especially if the words to explain it hadn't been invented yet? I always envision a bunch of people sitting around a boardroom table discussing what to name stuff:

"Mrs. Johnson, you have the floor," says the President.

"Thank you, Mr. McShake. I would like to propose a new word: 'abstract'" Mrs. Johnson proudly trumpets.

"Well, what does it mean?" says Board Member Number One.

76

"Well, that's just it, it kinda means 'conceptual, intangible, or something that isn't definable,' so in and of itself it's kind of a conundrum," Mrs. Johnson says to a confused boardroom.

"What's a conundrum?"

"I don't really know. Let's just figure that out later. Is the word approved?"

"Here here. It is so."

"Mr. McRib, you have the floor," the President once again chimes.

"Thank, you Mr. McShake. I would like to propose that we name that powdery stuff at the beach 'sand.' You know, that stuff that gets stuck between your toes and sometimes your rear end? I feel the word sand is appropriate due to the fact that it sounds like it could be fun and annoying at the same time. That seems to fit the description perfectly."

"Here here. It is so."

Most of you probably think that boardrooms weren't around way back when they were inventing words, but boardrooms have actually been around a lot longer than people think. By the time the Last Supper came around, boardrooms were a commonplace thing. In fact, the boardroom concept was actually invented in a boardroom. At least I think so. I kinda get confused 'cause I think of stuff like this when I'm on the toilet…and I'm an imbecile.

Chapter Fore

I'm a pretty observant person. Oh, not observant in the traditional sense of the word. I notice weird things. I guess since I've always kinda had my head in the clouds, I've been in a good vantage point to point out all the nitpicky silly things about life. Here are some of my recent observations:

1.)   I went into a public restroom and it had one of those never-ending cloth towel rolls (the never-ending ones that always seem to be at the end of the roll and are as filthy as a mechanic's shirt that hasn't been changed in months). It had a warning label that read:

> *- Use only to clean face and hands*
> *- Do not hang from towel*
> *- Intentional misuse can be harmful or fatal*

I found that label quite scary. First of all, I wouldn't clean *anything* with that towel, especially my face and hands; I'll drip-dry or use my pants, thank you very much. Secondly, I didn't realize that towel-hanging was such a common practice that it warranted putting it on a warning label. Third, short of cramming the towel down my throat or intentionally cutting it off the rack and hanging myself with it, I can't even think of any intentional misuse I could accomplish with a towel. And if I wanted to hurt myself, a dirty funky towel would not be my first choice of instrument. I guess the label is referring to a disease you might catch by actually using the towel—I could see that causing one harm.

2.)   There is Braille on the buttons of drive-thru ATM machines. You know, for all of those blind people driving around in cars or randomly walking up to drive-in ATM machines. I guess someone finally realized how stupid this was, since lately I've noticed that there are now headphone jacks on many ATM's (for all those blind people driving around in cars and randomly walking up to drive-through ATM machines). I've been tempted to plug a set of headphones into one of those jacks just to hear what they could possibly be saying on the other end.

ATTENDANT: "So let me get this straight, you're blind and you drove up to the ATM?"

BLIND PERSON: "No, silly, of course not. I just happened to be walking out in traffic and came upon this machine. So, naturally, I took out my headphones that I always carry around and started feeling around for a hole to plug them in."

I can only assume that there is someone talking on the other end, or there is a computer generated voice of some sort, because I think plugging in a set of headphones just to hear those beeping sounds that an ATM makes is a sure sign of insanity.

3.)   I noticed that my Dad's thermal lunch sack had the word "Sport" printed on the side of it. Naturally. Apparently anything that is made out of nylon and has Velcro on it is automatically proper for sports usage. I frequently see football players wearing bright blue and purple nylon fanny packs, and when is the last time you've seen an NBA game that doesn't have a player donning in a nylon-encased sports watch while adjusting the shoulder strap on his thermal sport drink cozy?

4.)   One of the ingredients in Mountain Dew is bromated vegetable oil. What the heck is that? When I used to work for a baked foods company, one of our selling points was that most of our breads and other baked goods no longer contained potassium bromate, which had been proven to cause cancer in lab animals (yes, I said *most* of our products no longer contained potassium bromate, not *all*...hmmm). I wonder if bromated vegetable oil is related to potassium bromate. Come to think of it, why is there vegetable oil in a drink?

Speaking of products causing cancer, saccharin (the main ingredient of Sweet & Low and other pink-packet sweeteners) has been proven to cause bladder cancer, yet for some reason it is still incredibly popular and has not been banned. Of course, cigarettes cause cancer and they haven't been banned either. Many people feel that your risk of cancer is only increased by saccharine after ingesting huge amounts of it, but studies have proven that if you drink on average only two drinks a day sweetened by saccharine, your bladder cancer risk is greatly increased.

Aspartame (the main ingredient of Nutrasweet, Equal, and other blue-packet sweeteners) has over ninety listed side effects including: headaches/migraines, dizziness, seizures, nausea, numbness, muscle spasms, weight gain, rashes, depression, fatigue, irritability, tachycardia, insomnia, vision problems, hearing loss, heart palpitations, breathing difficulties, anxiety attacks, slurred speech, loss of taste, tinnitus, vertigo, memory loss, and joint pain, and the following chronic diseases/conditions have been proven to be worsened by aspartame: brain tumors, multiple sclerosis, epilepsy, chronic fatigue syndrome, parkinson's disease, alzheimer's, mental retardation, lymphoma, birth defects, fibromyalgia, and diabetes. Man, I can't even pronounce some of those words, so I'm pretty sure I don't want any of those symptoms. If you're like me you noticed that diabetes was in that second list and weight gain was in the first one. Aren't those two of the main things people are trying to avoid by using aspartame in the first place?

The jury is still out on sucralose (Splenda). Splenda was supposed to be the superstar of the artificial sweetener gang. It's made from sugar so it supposedly tastes like sugar. However, what they fail to mention is that sucralose is made by chemically altering sugar by taking out three atoms of hydrogen/oxygen groups and replacing them with three atoms of chlorine groups. The result is a substance that is six-hundred times sweeter than sugar and can take stains out of your underwear. Alright, honestly the effect of the chlorine atom groups has still not been proven to be bad, that's why I said the jury's still out on this one. Much of our drinking water has chlorine in it and so does table salt for that matter.

Probably the most promising alternative to sugar is a newer product known as nocarbatall (marketed under the brand name Notasteatall). It is made by collecting the sweat from monkeys that are fed nothing but a strict low-carb diet. Okay, I'm just kidding about this one, but is it really so crazy when compared to the other three choices?

Tell me again why I should avoid sugar?

5.)	Almost all vienna sausages are rounded on the end and look like they've been cut off a longer vienna sausage. If they're rounded outward (convex) on the end, shouldn't there be some other vienna sausages that are rounded inward (concave)?

Vienna sausages have around 60 mg of cholesterol per can (around 20% of the recommended daily allowance). Something tells me it's not the "good" cholesterol.

6.)	Gojo makes a "Fine Italian Pumice" hand cleaner. Everyone knows Italian pumice is the best pumice. That's why Gojo only markets this product in the fanciest auto parts stores.

7.)	Every vacuum cleaner I've ever owned has had a light on the front of it. I've neither ever vacuumed in the dark, nor have ever detected more dirt via the light on the front of the vacuum cleaner.

8.)   I've never seen any horses playing.

9.)   The RadioShack logo is basically an R in a circle. Isn't that the symbol for "registered trademark?"

10.)   Regardless of what you eat at McDonald's, when you pass gas it always smells the same

11.)   On most Betty Crocker products that have ingredients separated into pouches, (such as Hamburger Helper, which has seasoning mix pouches) there are instructions that read: *Open at notch*. After opening somewhere in the neighborhood of two hundred of those packages over the last few years, I have only seen about three pouches that actually have a notch in them and don't require me biting the package open. Betty Crocker needs to recalibrate her notch-a-ma-jigger machine.

12.)   The words verb and adjective are nouns.

13.)   You can't sneeze with your eyes open…unless you don't have any eyelids.

14.)	Coffee made in a French coffee press is the bomb-diggity. Other things that qualify as the bomb-diggity: that cheese that comes in little wedges in a wooden wheel that has the laughing cow on it (what *is* she laughing about, anyway…what did she put in that cheese?), steamed crab legs, and Jazz music. Some would argue that Jesus belongs on this list, but He is on a much higher level of bomb-diggity-ness. Come on, you didn't think I'd put the Lord Almighty on the same list as the legs of a sea insect, did you?

15.)	If a person buys the most expensive computer on the market they probably have no idea how to use it, or they work for the government.

16.)	The US government had to upgrade their Minuteman Missiles with environmentally-friendly propulsion systems. Isn't the purpose of missiles to kill people and destroy stuff? I guess we don't want them developing cancer and dying in the three minutes it takes for the missile to arrive at its target.

17.)   Some Pepsi machines now take $1 *and* $2 bills. Thank goodness for that upgrade. Now I can spend the three $2 bills I've saved up over the last quarter-century or so.

18.)   There is an obscure law of physics that states that if a person spills a liquid, a large percentage of that liquid must land on said person's private area.

Chapter Fief

When Amee' and I first found out we were going to have our first son, we started telling everyone the good news. Naturally, we got the usual "congratulations" almost every time, but almost as regularly we were told "get ready for your life to change." Every time I heard that phrase, all I could think was, "of course my life is going to change. It changes when I buy a new pair of underwear. It changes every day. Obviously there is going to be a rather large change in my life when I have a child. No duh. Why does everyone find it necessary to tell me this?" Then Wilson was born. Then I realized why everyone told me that phrase so often.

Apparently, there are certain rules that you have to follow concerning kids. I'm not talking about the obvious, as in "feed them" and "don't kill them," I'm talking about rules such as the "legal disclaimer" rule.

The legal disclaimer rule refers to the aforementioned scenario in which everyone tells you that your life is going to change. By stating the obvious, those people have legally protected themselves from any action on your part. You can't even give those people a sarcastic, "hey, thanks for the heads up," after they have spoken the magic phrase.

The fact is, all the people that had been using the legal disclaimer rule on me typically either had children themselves or had been around people with children enough to realize how very much your life really does change. Like I stated before, the fact your life will change when you have children is obvious; the point people can't seem to get across to expectant parents is how *much* your life will change. There's just no good way to impress upon someone how much things change when you have a child. Thusly, you can cover yourself with a general "I told you so" statement, in the form of the legal disclaimer rule.

Rules concerning children don't stop with the legal disclaimer rule. Rules such as the legal disclaimer rule are to be followed by people when dealing with expectant parents. Other rules, such as the "your kid is a little punk, yet out of courtesy I have to discipline my child instead of whacking yours in the head" rule, are to be followed by the parents themselves. The "your kid is a little punk, yet out of courtesy I have to discipline my child instead of whacking yours in the head" rule, or the "little punk" rule for short, is one of my least favorites. This rule basically states that when someone else's child is being rude and trying to yank your kid's favorite toy out of his or her hand or boss your child around, rather than smack the little punk kid on the head or tell the parent off you're supposed to say something to the effect of, "Wilson, now be nice and share" until the parent of the other child finally calls off the little marauder.

Please don't think I'm talking about those occasions where your own kid is in the wrong or one of those "learn to share" moments—those are all well and good—the majority of the time I really feel my kids should share and be nice to other kids and be good Christians. I'm referring to those "terrorize the nursery" kids that just go from kid to kid with sticky "gimme" fingers while their parent just sits there smoking their cigarette or blankly staring into the clouds.

Who came up with this rule? Why is this considered common courtesy? One might argue that you're teaching your child to be good and share, but what about that other kid? All he's learning is that taking someone else's stuff is a-okay. Plus your kid is going to notice that the other kid is ending up on the apparent winning end and next time will want to *be* that kid.

Would this behavior be acceptable as an adult? Could you imagine if you were sitting down eating a sandwich and someone came by and snatched it out of your hands, but you couldn't do anything about it because your boss told you, "Rondreekay, now be nice and share?"

Of course not; if this happened in real life, you would stand up and deposit your tarsus into Mr. McSandwichGrabber's posterior (and possibly your boss'). At the very least you would verbally confront him.

Maybe the terms of the little punk rule should be changed to the following:

> 1.) If the little punk starts to take a toy away from your child, you have the right to say to the parent, "Excuse me, I'm sorry to disturb your smoke break and I understand you have issues with properly parenting your child, but my child was playing with that toy, which I happened to pay for with my money, and your child did not politely ask to borrow said toy. Due to this fact, and the fact that my child does not feel like sharing at this time, I will ask you to please remove your child from the general vicinity of my child, sans toy. If you fail to comply I reserve the right to invoke the little punk rule and allow my child to deposit his tarsus into your kid's posterior."

> 2.) If the little punk starts pushing your child around, you have the right to separate the two children without asking, and then proceed to push the parent of

the little punk directly into a wall or oncoming traffic, whichever is more convenient.

I think that would solve any issues with the current rule. There would have to be universal parent agreement on this one since some parents are bigger than other parents (i.e., the "my Daddy can beat up your Daddy" rule), so the larger parent would have to concede to the smaller when this rule is invoked.

Okay, for those of you that go to my church and are reading this I just need to point out that I'm not really very good at sarcasm and I'm *kidding* about the little punk rule, but you gotta admit, it'd be nice at times.

A rule that I've used quite often is the "just tired" rule. It's a simple one; basically, whenever your child starts pitching a fit and crying and/or screaming for no apparent reason, a parent can point out that their child is "just tired" and the child is due a nap. Other parents accept this, no questions asked, and know that you really mean, "I'm sorry about my kid being a little punk. I'll be sure to beat him/her senseless later when we're not in public."

A new rule that has snuck up on me over the last few Christmases and kids' birthdays is the "kid's toy packaging security overkill" rule.

Apparently toy theft is a bigger problem today then it was when I was a child, because practically every toy you buy nowadays is tied down to its cardboard packaging with no fewer than six wire ties and many times is screwed into the packaging as well.

Amee' bought a toy truck from the Dollar Tree (yup, for one dollar) and it was screwed into the cardboard box. Look, if a person is trying to steal a toy car from the Dollar Tree, that person has got other problems. Just let them have it.

The worst part about this rule isn't the fact that unwrapping these toys is so annoying; the worst part is having to sit through your child's impatience when you're trying to get it open for them. Usually they've just unwrapped a present and are ready to start playing with it, and then they have to sit through retarded Daddy trying to open up the present they just opened. My kids usually do a little jig that is reminiscent of the pee-pee dance that kids do when they have to go pee but won't admit it, all while asking "is it open yet?" or "are you done?" over and over on a repeating two-second delay.

Another rule I find disturbing is the Santa Claus rule. I was under the impression that lying to your children was wrong, but apparently if you lie about something that all the other parents are lying about, it's okay.

I decided to do a little research on 'Ole St. Nick to see if there was any rhyme and reason behind this rule enduring as long as it has. And the results of this research? Not much, actually. Seems the rule just kinda happened.

According to my research (which consisted of doing a search on Google while I was finishing up a cup of cappuccino), Santa Claus is a direct descendent of the Dutch legend of Sinter Klaas, which was actually a combination of many different legends as well as a real person, Bishop Nicholas of Smyrna (where modern day Turkey is). Bishop Nicholas, later dubbed Saint Nicholas by the Orthodox Church, was a real person who was well known for generously giving presents to the poor. Obviously he had to be a pretty spiffy fellow to be considered a Saint (*Interesting side note: St. Nick is the patron Saint of children, virgins, sailors, merchants, and thieves. Yes, thieves. Go figure*). His legend spread throughout Europe, and eventually to America, where it immediately became retardified and discombobulated. Parents got hold of the legend of Santa Claus and decided that the moral lesson of giving that he represented far outweighed the moral downside of lying to your children. The results of my research seem to indicate that those original Santa parents were hitting the absinthe a little hard.

I guess the parents that agreed on the Santa Claus rule forgot about the inevitable domino effect that occurs with any lie. Once you set the lie in motion, you keep having to create new lies to cover up your original lie.

So naturally, since children were involved, parents thought they could get by with any absurd lie they thought up. Thus, flying reindeer were invented. It wasn't too much of a stretch since the reindeer is an animal synonymous with flight. There was a problem with Santa getting into houses, so the parents just decided to say that a four-hundred pound fat man could squeeze down a chimney. To solve the problem of Santa's workforce, the task was assigned to elves. Not the arrow-shooting tail-kicking Lord of the Rings-type elves, but little gay midget elves with bright green outfits. And then came the house at the North Pole. I assume that one came about because the kids started asking why they couldn't ever see Santa during the year. Parents probably thought no kids would ever walk that far. Think about it, have you ever known an Eskimo kid who believed in Santa? Yes, somebody was hitting the absinthe *very* hard.

New lies just kept being created whenever the kids' "say what!?" factor would kick in. Take Rudolph, for example. Making a reindeer's nose glow bright red had to be the direct answer to a question like, "Mommy, but what happens when Santa is lost in the dark or the rain?"

The bad thing is that kids are getting smarter and the old lies don't always hold up. There is always that one smart kid that notices he doesn't have a chimney and the alarm would have gone off if Santa opened the door or window. A kid might even go so far as to say, "Hey! Santa must be thousands of years old! How can than be possible with him being so fat? Shouldn't he have had a heart attack? He's fatter than Uncle Rufus!" Rather than saying, "Good one, son. You got me. Yep, it's all one big fat lie. Let's go get some ice cream," the parents make the lie even more complex.

Some parents think they're pretty smart and actually find joy in making up the elaborate excuses to further confuse their kid. "Bobby, Santa is actually from a different dimension. He has the ability to phase shift and walk through solid matter. And don't even ask me how he can deliver presents to all the kids in the world. The fact is, there just aren't very many good kids anymore and the list is pretty short. Plus we can't even begin to understand other-dimensional beings. Let's go get some ice cream."

But, of course, there are more stupid parents than smart ones, and usually they blurt out something like: "Santa used to be a cat burglar. He's good at sneaking into windows. And he'll kill you if you ask any more questions." Nowadays real absinthe is mostly illegal, so parents mostly rely on whiskey.

I'm dreading the time when my children are old enough for the "big lie." On one hand, I have absolutely no desire to lie to them. On the other hand, if I don't tell the story of Santa Claus to them as "truth," I would still have to let them know about it so their friends at school won't get their feelings hurt (or worse, hurt *my* kids' feelings…or face when they get punched) when my kids call them complete and utter morons. Then I would still have to bribe them to keep them from telling all their classmates the real truth and having their parents get upset at me. I don't know if I have enough candy to do that.

I guess this is where home schooling comes in. Heck, my wife was home schooled up until High School and turned out a lot less weird than I did. But then again, she did marry me. One can't be too sane to do something like that. She probably ordered some absinthe online.

If I have to go through with the Santa Claus rule, I'm going to suggest a few changes. But, to be fair to other parents, I'll try out the new rules on my own children before turning in my suggestions to the Worldwide Child Rule Council.

First of all, I'm going to tell my children that they are going to be entrusted with a big secret. I'll tell them that all of the kids in the world are told the story of Santa Claus because they lack the mental capacity to understand the real truth. Only a select few really really smart kids could be let in on the secret. In fact, if the most kids knew the real truth their heads would explode.

The smart kids can't ever tell all the stupid kids the truth out of moral obligation. And just in case Jacob gets the bright idea that exploding people's heads is easier and more fun than whack-a-mole (see Chapter Juan), I'll tell them that it's a two-way street—if they are responsible for someone else's head exploding, a Christmas Ninja will chop the responsible kid's head off too.

In my version of the truth, the Santa Claus role will be replaced by none other than SuperFlyer (see Chapter Tree). I wouldn't have to explain how SuperFlyer could possibly deliver all the presents in one night; SuperFlyer has the speed and strength to pull it off, so the answer would be obvious. I'll tell them that SuperFlyer is just starting the job this year, as he has recently inherited it from his dad, SuperWalker. SuperFlyer is a little meaner than his dad and will actually go one step further than just putting kids on a "good" and "bad" list—he'll visit bad kids' homes and burn off one of their toes with his heat vision. In the case of a child that has no toes, he'll move to fingers. Children that are both toeless and fingerless are exempt from this policy, but just to show that being handicapped isn't an excuse for being a little punk, the only presents that SuperFlyer will give them are things like pianos or squirt guns or anything else that requires phalanges for full enjoyment. And SuperFlyer might just go ahead and pluck them really hard on the nose for good measure.

Then SuperFlyer would give me the money that he would have spent on their presents and will only let me spend it on dorky clothes that they have to wear to school. See, in order to avoid that fate, you'll get year-long good behavior from your kids.

Finally, when my kids get to the age that all their friends have finally figured out the truth about Santa, I'll remind them that the exploding head thing is still in effect, and SuperFlyer would no longer be bringing them presents since for one second they actually contemplated that he wasn't real, and I would be morally obliged to tell SuperFlyer. But since they had been so good over the years, he wouldn't come and fry off a toe. Unless they wreck my car, then it's barbequed piggy time. Where'd I put that bottle of whiskey?

Chapter Sicks

Coffee is yet another bit of proof that God exists. Atheists have obviously never had a really good cup of coffee. They probably just drink instant. Upon taking a sip of a really really good cup of coffee, I'm sure an atheist would exclaim "Dear Lord!" and proceed to repenting at an altar.

I'm not sure exactly when my obsession with coffee began, but it probably goes back to when I was a kid and my Mom would give me coffee mixed in a 1 coffee : 2 cream : 2 sugar ratio. Also, around that same time I was living in Okinawa, Japan, where they sell coffee popsicles and coffee candy.

There are unfounded rumors floating around that coffee is bad for you and it can cause health problems, but I'm sure that can't be true. I think short term memory loss might be one of the so-called symptoms, but I just can't remember.

There are unfounded rumors floating around that coffee is bad for you and it can cause health problems, but I'm sure that can't be true. I think short term memory loss might be one of the so-called symptoms, but I just can't remember.

Coffee's history dates back prior to 1000 AD. Here are some of the more interesting points:

c800 AD	An Ethiopian goat herder named Kaldi finds his goats dancing around a shrub. The goat herder samples the cherries from the shrub and notes that they make him "happy."
c1000 AD	Africans make primitive "energy bars" by wrapping coffee beans up in animal fat. Mmmm, delectable!
1475 AD	The world's first coffee shop opens in Constantinople. Turkish law at the time declares that a woman can divorce her husband if he doesn't provide her with her daily quota of coffee.
1607 AD	John Smith brings coffee to the new world. Some Canadian historians claim that it arrived earlier in

Canada but naturally, like most things, they're wrong.

1652 AD   Coffeehouses known as "Penny Universities" (since a penny was typically the price of admission—not really sure about the University part) open up in England. Interestingly enough, the number of inventions and innovations in England skyrockets, as it does around the world as more and more coffeehouses are introduced. It could be coincidence, but I doubt it. Also around this time the word "TIPS," standing for "To Insure Prompt Service," was developed in an English coffeehouse, which hundreds of years later developed into a practice that my friend Shawn Mitchell refuses to take part in (tipping, that is, not coffee drinking).

1688 AD	Edward Lloyd opens up his coffeehouse, which later becomes Lloyd's of London, currently one of the world's best known insurance companies.
1773 AD	American colonials realize that coffee is superior to tea and make coffee drinking a patriotic duty, consummated by the Boston Tea Party.
1901 AD	Instant coffee is invented by a Japanese-American chemist, Satori Kato, who is clearly insane or under the effect of heavy hallucinogens.
1903 AD	German Ludwig Roselius, clearly insane or under the effect of heavy hallucinogens, gives coffee beans to researchers to develop the first decaffeinated coffee, Sanka.

1942 AD   Packets of coffee are issued in American WWII soldiers' ration kits, once again proving America is the greatest country in the world.

1976 AD   Tony Marshall is born. World coffee consumption booms.

Like I said earlier, I don't know exactly when my obsession began, but if I had to pick a particular moment that it got out of control it would have to be one day in college during my Freshman year at Mississippi State University: my friend Jeff Foster was working at a frozen yogurt shop in Columbus, Mississippi and me and my roommate, Zack Shoemake, had come by early to get our daily free "samples" and to get Jeff to punch the holes out of our free yogurt punch cards to use during the times when he wasn't working. To this day I wish Jeff never quit that job. While we were there I drank several cups of coffee from the complimentary coffee maker.

Later, when we got back to our dorm room we decided to fire up Zack's relatively new "free" 4-cup coffeemaker that he got as a gift for joining a mail-order coffee club and signing his soul away over the next several months.

Several, several, cups of coffee later Zack and I got the bright idea (probably at this point implanted by evil coffee pixies) to invite a couple of friends over and have a coffee party. We weren't really sure what a coffee party was, except that it involved coffee, shortbread cookies, and…well, that's about it.

So our mutual friend from high school, Dana, and her roommate, Laura, came over and we all drank coffee and ate shortbread cookies until around 3AM.

From the time I started drinking coffee at the yogurt shop until the time Dana and Laura left I consumed somewhere in the neighborhood of eighteen cups of coffee.

At 3AM I finally remembered that I had a project of some sort due that morning in my 8AM class. I say some sort of project because I can't remember if it was a paper or a speech I had to prepare. I'm surprised I remembered anything from that night/morning.

So after drinking a few more cups of coffee to keep me awake while starting and finishing my paper/speech, I crashed for an hour or so, went to class, and then continued to consume coffee pretty much non-stop after that.

Zack, aka "the more sensible roommate," didn't suffer as many of the same aftereffects that I did, but did occasionally jump on the coffee insanity boat with me.

Since that one fateful day/night/day, I have been a member of numerous coffee clubs, owned several different coffee makers and cappuccino machines, roasted my own green coffee beans, and drank enough coffee to fill the gap that God made for Moses through the Red Sea.

It's pretty needless to say that I really like coffee, but there are others in the world that are much more obsessive than me. Coffee is actually the number two commodity in the world (number one being oil), with more than 400 billion cups being consumed each year.

For the utterly obsessed connoisseur, there is the most expensive coffee in the world, Kopi Luwak.

Sporting a $175-300 per pound price tag, Kopi Luwak is no casual coffee drinker's coffee. As you may have guessed from its hefty cost, Kopi Luwak is very rare, with only 500 or so pounds being produced every year—mostly purchased by the Japanese. I don't know why I felt it necessary to point out that this coffee is mostly purchased by Japanese people; for some reason I just find that fact funny. There's some humor in there that I just can't quite pinpoint.

Kopi Luwak is special for another reason besides its price and rarity. What gives Kopi

Luwak its unique taste is the fact that the final product has actually been digested by a small animal known as the palm civet (scientific name is paradoxurus hermaphroditus, for all you science nerds), a relative of the housecat.

The palm civet supposedly eats only the ripest and reddest coffee cherries, which also happen to be the best ones to gather and roast. The animal removes the fleshy meat of the cherries and the beans pass through its system whole and supposedly "clean." I guess not clean in the traditional sense, but maybe clean like a hitchhiking hippie who claims to be "free".

I've never tried any Kopi Luwak, and would probably never attempt to get any of the beans, but honestly if someone were to offer me a cup, I'd probably try it…once. Unless it's akin to the Spice Melange in the Dune novels, I don't think I'll try a second cup though.

Do I think it is worth the $175-300 per pound price tag? I guess that's up to the market, and since the few pounds of it that are produced every year are eagerly snatched up as quickly as they are produced, I rectum so.

Chapter Sicks plus Juan

When referring to college and/or po' folks cuisine, the basic food groups are different than the traditionally accepted FDA "food triangle". The usual meat, fruits & vegetables, grains, and dairy groups are replaced by Cheese and/or imitation cheese sauce, Macaroni and Noodles, Condiments, Fast Food, and Pizza. Another way of organizing these foods would be "convenient," "cheap," and "really cheap," but many times those groups can overlap.

I think that everyone should attend college for at least a little while, not so much for the classroom education, but for the survival skills you pick up from being a broke and hungry college student—and let's face it; a lot of folks post-college are just broke and hungry college graduates. Not only do you learn how to survive off very little, but your creative side also flourishes as you attempt to make something edible out of items such as packets of ketchup and chocolate syrup.

However, in order to aid in the process, I've devised a po' folks/college cookbook, as well as a few guidelines regarding college food:

Guideline #1: Obtain a mini-fridge or access to a refrigerator. If it's the latter, make sure you have some way of keeping others out of your food. Zipper storage bags with a biohazard symbol on the side are a good way of ensuring this. The reason you need a fridge is because you *will* be eating leftovers, regardless if you liked the original meal or not.

Guideline #2: Obtain a way to boil water, whether it is an electric water boiling pot or a hotplate. Most dorms don't allow either of these so a disguise might be necessary to throw pesky resident assistants off the trail. I would suggest setting aside a "craft day" to design functional yet decorative disguises, ala Martha Stewart…on second thought, nah, just hide them under your bed after they cool off. If all else fails you can always just superheat water in the microwave and pray it doesn't explode in your face. This brings us to guideline #3…

Guideline #3: Obtain a microwave. The reasons for this one should be obvious.

Guideline #4: Stuff as much plastic ware and as many napkins as you can in your pockets and/or backpack every time you pass through the food court, cafeteria, or any other eating establishment for that matter. Plastic is the key

110

word here…for two reasons: One, you don't
want to have to wash them; two, you don't want
to go to jail for stealing silverware someone
might not want to give away.

Guideline #5: Know which days the local
burger joints have specials. Me and Zack's
favorite was 33¢ mini-burger day at Sonic. This
is another reason to have a refrigerator. Sure,
eating the same burgers every day over and over
can get kinda boring, but that's where guideline
#6 and some of the recipes come into effect.

Guideline #6:   Save as many condiments
from restaurants that you can so you can change
the flavor of your refrigerated leftovers.

Guideline #7: Never hand a pizza delivery
person a coupon for a pizza until they actually
ask you for the coupon. They rarely do, so you
can save the coupon and the next time you order
you don't have to lie when you tell them you
have a coupon. Also, even if your coupons are
expired just tell the person on the phone you
have a coupon; don't mention the expiration
date. Very seldom will they ever ask if the
coupon is expired or not, and then when the
delivery person gets there just do as above —
don't hand them the coupon until they ask.

Chances are that even if they do ask they won't know what to do if they notice it's expired.

Guideline #8: Buy sliced cheese, sour cream, and the like from the grocery store and skip out on adding those items to your fast food meals via the menu at the standard restaurant markup of one billion percent, unless you're a guy and you're just trying to impress a date. Nothing makes an impact on a lady like a big sour cream spender.

Guideline #9: If you absolutely must purchase a drink from a fast food restaurant, make sure you get the smallest size and just get the free refills. If they charge for refills, get a larger size and ask for no ice. Drinks come out of the fountain refrigerated anyway. If you absolutely must have ice cold drinks, try to not drink anything until winter time, when it's naturally cold out.

Guideline #10: If you're almost totally broke, but closing in on your next payday/visit home to your parents, consider using those last few coins you've dug up from the cracks of the couch by going to an all-you-can eat buffet and staying there all day. This would be a great time to catch up on homework or writing that stupid novel you've always wanted to write. Sure, you'll miss all your classes that day, but what's more important, getting an education or staying alive? Studies prove you don't really learn much on an empty stomach anyway. If the Oriental and/or Indian and/or Mexican person that owns the restaurant gets mad at you and tries to kick you out, demand a refund. You probably won't get one, but it might be fun to see the reaction.

Guideline #11: Consider making friends with someone who works at a frozen yogurt store, or bullying one of your friends into working at one.

Guideline #12: Forget about going on a low-carb diet. Leave that for later in life when you have to sit in a cubicle all day long and your metabolism slows down to a snail's pace. Your diet in college will mostly consist of some sort of pasta or dough product, which all contain about 833% carbohydrates, so just forget about joining the new diet revolution.

That should lay some groundwork for you. On to the recipes:

Cheesy Ramen Noodles

A twist on the traditional ramen noodle diet of college students everywhere.

Ingredients:

1-2 packages of Ramen Noodles *(whatever brand is cheapest)*

Some type of cheese (American singles, cheddar cheese block, easy squeeze cheese, or if you're desperate, powdered cheese flavored sauce or cheese soup mix in a can)

Instructions:

Boil some water. Add just the noodles from the ramen noodle packages (save the flavoring packages for later. You'll probably never use them, but they count as a food product and you don't throw away any type of food product unless it has mold or rat bites on it…and even then salvage as much of it as possible). When noodles are at the desired consistency, remove them from boiling water and place in a bowl. Ramen noodles can be eaten raw, so don't worry about undercooking them, just cook them until they look "right." Immediately add as much cheese as you'd like to spare while noodles are still hot. I personally prefer easy squeeze cheese because, well, it's easy, but it's also kinda pricey and about as addictive as crack cocaine so you'll end up using up the canister in no time. Stir until cheese is melted (or mixed in the case of easy squeeze cheese). Add a single-use black pepper package if desired, taking care to open package first and not add the paper, only the pepper. Eat cheesy noodles. Proclaim, "Mmmm, cheesy noodles." Take nap. Run 5 miles to work off all of those carbs you just ate.

Ramen Noodle push-up

For those on-the-go (i.e., late for class) students, consider the easy to make ramen noodle push-up.

Ingredients:

1 package of ramen noodles *(whatever brand is cheapest)*

Instructions:

Carefully open ramen noodle package on one end and remove flavoring package. Save flavoring package for later. Slide noodle block up from the bottom of package, exposing the top portion of the noodle block. Eat noodle block, sliding it up as you consume it until it is gone. Proclaim, "Mmmm, hard crunchy noodle goodness." Go to class and fail test. Take nap. Run 5 miles to work off all those carbs you just ate.

Lunch Meat push-up

This one is just like the ramen noodle push-up, but replace the package of ramen noodles with a package of el-cheapo processed lunch meat (they're usually around 50¢ per package…look on the label for the brand with the highest amount of sodium and you've probably found the correct one). After eating proclaim, "Mmmm, salty meaty goodness," and take an extra long sodium-coma nap instead of a short nap and a run.

Extra-cheesy Bowl of Cheese

This one might be a little pricier, so it qualifies under the "convenient" category, but if you're a cheese lover, this one is for you.

Ingredients:

1 package of shredded cheese (*any flavor, whatever you prefer…I like the mixed Colby and Jack…Muenster is good too, but mostly because it's just fun to say*)

1-2 slice(s) of cheese singles (*any flavor, now that in this great day and age they have multiple cheese singles flavors…what a country we live in!*)

Instructions:

Pour shredded cheese into a bowl until the bowl is mostly full. Top off shredded cheese with 1-2 slice(s) of cheese singles. Place bowl in microwave and cook just long enough for the grease to start coming out of the shredded cheese (usually just a few seconds, microwaves vary so keep a close eye on it). Remove bowl. Eat cheese with bare hands. Proclaim, "Mmmm, slightly melted cheesy cheese." Take nap with huge smile on face.

Ketchup Mustard Bread

Really broke? Can you afford a loaf of bread? Then you're eating, Brotha!

Ingredients:

1 loaf of el-cheapo bread *(by the private label, i.e., store-brand, bread…I worked for a bread company for 3 years, TRUST ME, it's all pretty much the same if not EXACTLY the same as the expensive stuff, the only difference being that the wrappers on private label are typically much thinner and thusly the bread goes bad faster—not a problem if you either eat the bread quickly or get a plastic breadbox to keep it fresh)*

Several single-use packets of ketchup and mustard

Instructions:

Open several single-use packages of ketchup and mustard and mix together in a bowl. Dip slices of bread in ketchstard and eat dipped slices. Proclaim,

"Mmmm, rib eye steak," in an attempt to
trick yourself into believing you're not
eating bread dipped in ketchup and
mustard. Take long nap and lucidly
dream of rib eyes and New York strips.

Variations on this recipe include using
taco sauce or salsa for a spicy kick, or
pancake syrup, which many times comes
in a convenient dipping container.

Goober Grape Surprise

Ah, Goober Grape, the lazy man's peanut
butter and jelly. Who has time to open
two jars? Thanks to comedian Brian
Regan for giving me the idea for this one.

Ingredients:

1 jar of Goober Grape or any other brand
of pre-mixed peanut butter & jelly

1-3 packages of croutons from the salad
bar section of a fast food restaurant

Instructions:

Eat enough of the Goober Grape to make
enough room for the croutons. Dump

desired amount of croutons in Goober
Grape jar. Stir together until thouroghly
mixed. Enjoy your all-in-one peanut
butter and jelly sandwich mix. Proclaim,
"Mmmm, peanutty sticky sweet and
crunchy goodness with no extra cleanup."
Sleep tight. Don't let the bed bugs bite.

Zackatony and Cheese

Here it is, the big daddy of all college
recipes. One of my college roommates,
Zack Shoemake, and I stumbled upon this
recipe when attempting to make macaroni
and cheese by following the steps on the
side of the box, which included adding
milk (which we surprisingly had) and
butter (which we did not have).
Determined to find some source of butter
without having to actually leave our
dorm room, our eyes happened upon the
stack of unused garlic butter dipping
sauce from Papa John's Pizza that we had
due to our rule of never throwing away a
food product. The garlic butter dipping
sauce containers back then were the exact
size of the amount of butter the macaroni
and cheese instructions called for, so we
decided "what the heck?" and threw it in
the mix. The result was so tasty that we

assigned our own names to it, and a classic was born.

Ingredients:

1 box of macaroni and cheese *(I admit that the Kraft brand is probably the best, but when you add the special ingredient, it doesn't matter too much. Go for the cheapest unless the Kraft isn't much more expensive)*

2 packages of Papa John's garlic butter dipping sauce *(this is actually a guesstimate; back when I was in college one package was the perfect size, but nowadays the packages are about half the size. If you don't have any extras lying around, Papa John's will sell you extra sauce or just sauce with no pizza if needs be. Me and Zack once ordered nothing but garlic sauce and drinks and just ordered enough to meet their minimum delivery amount.)*

Instructions:

Make macaroni and cheese according to instructions on side of box, with the exception of using the Papa John's garlic butter dipping sauce in lieu of the butter that the instructions call for. If you can't follow the instructions on the side of the box, find someone to show you how to make it, since macaroni and cheese preparation is one of the essential skills a college student must master. Check your school's course catalogue; there may be a class they offer on it. Eat Zackatony and cheese. Proclaim, "Mmmm, I am in heaven." Take a long nap in total bliss. Skip out on the 5 mile run, the Zackatony and Cheese was worth the extra carbs, no need to punish yourself.

Chapter Ate

Have you ever heard of that game, the Six Degrees of Kevin Bacon?   If not, lemme enlighten you.   Kevin Bacon has been in over fifty movies and had well over thirty television appearances.   He has also had a hand in producing numerous movies and programs and is a member of a musical band with his brothers. One day some college students from Pennsylvania noticed the fact that Kevin has worked with so many different people in show business, and so they devised a game called the Six Degrees of Kevin Bacon. The premise of the game is that you can connect any person in entertainment to Kevin Bacon within only six steps. Many folks can be connected in less than six steps, but it shouldn't take more than six. Confused? Discombobulated? Let me give you an example:

Let's say you wanted to see if Kevin was six degrees away from our favorite guy-that-always-talks-like-he's-drunk, Sylvester Stallone.

So:

1.) Sylvester Stallone who was in Demolition Man with:
2.) Rob Schneider who was in The Hot Chick with:
3.) Anna Farris who was in Scary Movie 3 with:
4.) Charlie Sheen who was in Young Guns with:
5.) Kiefer Sutherland who was in Flatliners with:
6.) KEVIN BACON

Okay, so that one might have been too easy since Sylvester Stallone has been in several movies himself. That being said though, using computer calculations, the University of Virginia (who has a neat website that automatically determines an actor's "Bacon Number" at www.oracleofbacon.org) estimates that only 12% of actors can't be linked with Kevin through *movies only*, and it's usually because they've only been in TV-only movies that their database doesn't include.

Most (almost all that I tried) actors and actresses seem to link up with Kevin in less than six degrees. I even tried a lot of Indian Bollywood actresses and all of them linked within three steps.

I've heard that if you lax your criteria a bit, you can link just about anyone in the world within six or seven degrees.

I'm assuming when they say lax your criteria, they don't mean something like: "Tony Marshall is a human, Kevin Bacon, too, is a human. Bacon number of one." I decided to experiment this theory and here are a few that I came up with.

I'll start with an easy one:

Tom Hanks → Tony Marshall

1.) Tom Hanks was in Apollo 13 which was directed by:
2.) Ron Howard who was on Happy Days with:
3.) Henry Winkler who once visited Okinawa, Japan with the cast of Happy Days and got his picture taken with:
4.) TONY MARSHALL

I'm sure getting his picture taken with me was the highlight of his career. Coincedentally, Garry Marshall was the director of Happy Days, and his father is Mork and Mindy producer Tony Marshall.

Okay, let's try another one, this time not using my Fonz connection:

SpongeBob SquarePants → Tony Marshall

1.) SpongeBob SquarePants, voiced by Tom Kenny, is on his own show, SpongeBob SquarePants, which sometimes stars:
2.) Tim Conway (as the voice of Barnacleboy) who was in the Apple Dumpling Gang with:
3.) Don Knotts, who was on The Andy Griffith Show with:
4.) Andy Griffith, who is a member of Phi Mu Alpha Sinfonia music fraternity, to which:
5.) TONY MARSHALL is also a member

Perhaps now my kids will respect me, knowing my connection to SpongeBob.

Time for a tougher one:

Saddam Hussein → Tony Marshall

1.) Saddam Hussein was ousted from Iraq due to:
2.) George W. Bush who is the son of:
3.) George Bush, Sr., who was the Vice President of:
4.) Ronald Reagan, who once stopped at a McDonalds and ate, and the table at

which he sat at got a special memorial cover denoting that he ate there, and that table was later used by:
5.) TONY MARSHALL

That I can be connected to Saddam Hussein is not a proud point for me, but I guess it proves that the idea that you can connect yourself to just about anyone is true. Considering my grandmother's last name was Smith, I'm probably related to half the people in America in some way or another anyway. My grandfather on my mother's side's last name was Nguyen, which means I'm also probably related to half the people in Vietnam. And of course, you can go back as far as Adam and Eve and well, you get the point.

There's also the popular theory that everyone has an identical double somewhere in the world, whether it just be a look-a-like or an evil twin. I find the concept of me having an evil twin hard to believe for two reasons: 1.) That's just too much handsome for one planet, and 2.) I can't grow a goatee correctly, and since an evil twin is supposed to be physically identical to the good twin (albeit EVIL), I cannot have an evil twin since everyone knows that all evil twins have a goatee. If the good twin already has a goatee, the evil twin has a really long Chinese-movie type goatee to prove its superior evilness.

The identical double theory is also hard for me to believe, but only for reason number one that I listed earlier.

I've also heard of the concept of a doppelganger. I always thought a doppelganger was some sort of German word meaning evil twin, but I found this definition of doppelganger on the internet:

Meaning "double walker," a doppelganger is a shadow-self that accompanies every human. Only the owner of a doppelganger can see it, otherwise it is invisible to human eyes. Dogs and cats have been known to see doppelgangers. Providing sympathetic company, a doppelganger almost always stands behind a person, and they cast no reflection in a mirror. They are prepared to listen and give advice to humans, either implanting ideas in their heads, or a sort of osmosis. It is said to be bad luck if it is seen, and rarely a doppelganger will make itself visible to friends or family, often causing great confusion. Doppelgangers can be mischievous and malicious.

You know what? People are nuts. That definition pretty much says to me: Doppelganger = YOUR SHADOW and/or YOUR CONCIENCE. Someone schizophrenic looked at his shadow one day and started talking to himself and convinced himself that no one else could see his shadow. Then a dog barked at the

128

shadow and Mr. Mcwhack-job decided that "ruff ruff" translates into "hey, crazy, I see your shadow and it is obviously a mischievous and malicious creature that is the reason for all the bad stuff you do." It's convenient that usually only the owner can see a doppelganger and that it is rarely ever visible by friends and family. The friends and family that can see it are probably certifiable as well.

I've got some pretty weird stuff going on inside my head, but I don't believe I ever came up with something on par with the definition of a doppelganger. But I can try…

You know when you're in a large room or standing over a canyon and you yell something, and then a few seconds later you hear the same thing you yelled repeated back to you? Well, that's your repeatamajanger.

A repeatamajanger is a creature that resides in large rooms or canyons and is basically the "yes man" of the mysterious creature world. Their sole purpose is to verify everything you yell so you feel reassured and better about yourself, regardless if your statement was the stupidest thing ever uttered on the face of the earth.

Like doppelgangers, repeatamajangers are usually unseen. Unlike doppelgangers, a repeatamajanger makes its comments known to everyone within yelling distance, since you always feel better if someone else knows that others agree with you.

So the next time your so-called friends are making fun of you and telling you your ideas are stupid, take them to a large canyon and yell your ideas to your repeatamajanger. If your "friends" still don't agree with you, you can always just push them into the canyon.

Chapter Nein

$\mathbf{A}$s you now know if you read Chapter Fore, I am a very observant person. Being an observant person does have its drawbacks though; with noticing many things comes many questions. Unfortunately the answers don't always come with those questions.

Sometimes finding those answers can be a rewarding experience. Other times, finding those answers will make one want to rip their hair out, which in my bald-headed case is quite difficult.

I've decided to list some of those more perplexing questions here. Yes, I know some of my observations in Chapter Fore were followed by questions; you get the observant little smarty-pants award if you wanted to point that out—stop pointing out stuff to yourself while you're reading a book, your other personality will think you're crazy.

So without further ado, I give you my list of questions that make me want to pull my non-existent hair out:

1.)   Why do people brush their teeth before they go to the dentist? Do they think that one brushing is going to make up for all the hundreds of brushings they missed, and that the dentist will be fooled? Let's say you have a dumb dentist and you actually did "fool" him/her…don't you run the risk of not getting a good cleaning if they don't think you need a thorough one? I used to date a girl who's Dad made her clean the house before the cleaning ladies came each week, so they wouldn't think they were a bunch of slobs. If I hired people to clean my house, I'd be the exact opposite, I'd want them to know how much of a slob I am so they would feel appreciated. See, I care about people's feelings. I want a dentist to look into my mouth, gag, and tell his hygienist, "let's give him the works!" That's why I don't brush for 3 months before I go to the dentist.

2.) How can a household cleaner rightfully be called an "all-purpose cleaner/degreaser?"

Isn't being a degreaser just one purpose? If it truly is all-purpose, wouldn't that encompass degreasing as well? If so, then why do you find all-purpose cleaners *and* all-purpose degreasers made by the same company? I'm assuming all-purpose only refers to cleaning, and not actually every purpose on the face of the earth. I never read anything in the Bible about being able to baptize someone with a bottle of 409.

3.) On Sci-Fi TV shows that have the main cast separated from their home world for extended periods of time (i.e., Star Trek, Stargate: Atlantis, etc.), do they bring a hairdresser with them? Usually the crews don't seem to have standard military-issue hairdos. I notice this because I was once relegated to a military-issue hairdo, and because I have no hair now and am envious of all that do have hair. Well, not really, but by writing that I am able to up the word count of my book, thusly increasing the overall price of it. There…I did it again…and again…

4.) Why do some fast food restaurants charge extra for condiments (excluding college towns…see Chapter Sicks plus Juan for the reason behind that one)? Is giving away too many condiments really that big of a problem? At the company meeting, do they say: "well, we had record sales this month— sales on Floofy Burgers have gone up 800%! If we could only cut down on the .0001¢ we lose every time we give away an extra packet of Floofy Sauce or the .000000001¢ we lose every time we give away an extra packet of mustard, that would put us over the top!" …and then they decide to charge 30¢ a pack to make up for it.

5.) Why do both Dr. Phil (a fat man) and his son (a fat young man) both have best-selling diet books? That's like me selling a hair-growing book…and being really successful at it.

6.) Is it possible for a person confined to a wheelchair to be a stand-up comedian?

7.) When Microsoft released Service Pack 2 for Windows XP, it included a pop-up blocker add-on to their internet explorer web browser. This was a good thing, since pop-up ads are incredibly annoying. However, what made Microsoft think that a pop-up message explaining that it just blocked a pop-up advertisement would be any less annoying?

8.) If products labeled as "extreme" (such as Extreme Nachos, or X-treme Thirst Quencher, or Extremely X-treme Hemorrhoid cream) one day take up the majority of the market, would they cease to be "extreme?"

9.) Why do people preface a pointless statement with "it goes without saying" and then go ahead and say it anyway?

10.) I DJ'ed at a college radio station one summer. It was a volunteer job and I had a paying job that I had to get to immediately after my DJ shift ended. The problem was the girl that came in after me, Melinda, never felt it was necessary to get there on time, thusly making me late for my paying job almost every week. There was a phone in the DJ booth that had a flasher on it instead of a ringer, so it wouldn't ring out loud while you were talking on the air. Most people didn't realize you could turn the flasher off and the phone would ring. My questions are: Did Melinda ever figure out it was me who called her on the phone every single time she got on the air so the phone would ring loudly and mess her up? *and* After the tenth or so time I did it, why didn't she just take the phone off the hook whenever she was about to go on the air?

11.)   Why do so many movies that are really bad eventually become "classics?"

12.)   I don't understand the correct usage of "pre." As in, pre-registering for college classes. Doesn't that mean you register before you register? Pre-paying for something…does that mean you have to pay twice? I'm discombobulated…or is it pre-discombobulated?

13.)   Why do men's restrooms always have a bunch of urinals lined up next to each other so closely? No man wants to use one right next to another man, so there's always an unused urinal between each person. Most men will either wait for one person to move or just use a regular toilet before using a urinal right next to another man. The exception of course is sporting events, in which you're just trying to use the bathroom as quickly as possible so you still have time to hit the concession stand before halftime is over. That's why most sports stadiums just have a big trough instead of separate urinals. My solutions for normal restrooms would be a.) leave a huge space between each urinal and still have those dividers, b.) keep the current configuration of urinals, but increase the size of the dividers to go from the bottom of the floor all the way up to the ceiling, as well as an extra foot or so out from the wall, or c.) put each urinal on a different wall. The last one might be tricky in a smaller bathroom and might require designing rooms in an irregular polygonal format.

14.)   If flying is statistically safer than driving, then why are you required to have hours and hours of flight time to get a pilots license and only have to take a ten minute test to get a driver's license? I guess that explains the reason flying is statistically safer than driving.

15.)   Was the Bible referring to a
         low-carb diet when it said
         "…not by bread alone…?"

16.)   Why did all the old 80's
         cartoons always end with
         someone telling a cheesy joke
         or making a cheesy statement
         and then everyone laughing?

*HERO #1: "Wow, we barely
escaped with our lives. We should
all be dead right now. That huge
monster/alien/robot just hacked all
the hair off my head…I'm lucky it
wasn't my whole head!"*

*HERO #2: "Well, at least you got
a free hair cut!"*

*ALL HEROES: "Ha ha ha ha ha
ha ha ha ha ha ha ha ha!!"*

Roll credits

17.)   Why does Microsoft Word
         always underline words that
         you type two or more times in a
         row (indicating that every word
         after the original is spelled
         incorrectly) as in, "Ha ha ha ha
         ha ha ha ha ha ha ha ha!!"

Chapter Tin

In case my writing style wasn't pointless and random enough for you, I thought I would go ahead and put in this last chapter for you in order to cover all the bases. This is the chapter that I threw everything else that I couldn't seem to fit in any other category. Some of it is old writings from way back when, some of it is from my blog at www.boombasticninja.us, and some of it is just new stuff.

The Chinese Refill Donut

I debated including this in the college cookbook section of the book, but realized that this recipe isn't quite practical for most college students, since deep-frying isn't always part of the college skill set, and I didn't feel like going into detailed instructions on how to deep fry something.

Have you seen those "Chinese donuts" you can get at most Chinese buffets? You know, the ones that don't have a hole in the middle and are covered in sugar? Well, my Mom showed me the secret to making those.

Chinese donuts are simply deep-fried biscuit dough (the sweeter kinds of dough work better). You pop open a can of Pillsbury biscuits, deep fry them to a golden brown, sprinkle with either regular or powdered sugar, and proceed to devour them and do the proclaiming "Mmmm" thing as described in chapter Sicks plus Juan.

Me and my college roommate, Zack, found an interesting use for the Chinese donut: one day we were dining at a local Chinese buffet and noticed that the waitress kept refilling only one of our glasses at a time, regardless of the level of liquid in our glasses.

We were both drinking the same thing, so we found the waitress' behavior kind of odd. After a little detective work, we determining that whoever had a Chinese donut sitting out in plain view of the waitress got drink refills, while the other did not, hence the name, "Chinese refill donut."

We tested this theory several times and it usually was right on the mark; whenever we both had a donut we both got refills, when only one had a donut only that person would get a refill, etc. etc.

I suggest you try out the Chinese refill donut theory yourself and you too will discover one of two things: that either the Chinese refill donut theory is correct and should be referred to as "law" and not "theory," or that you're gullible enough to try anything.

US Senator Humor

I don't count this as talking about politics, but if you read this and feel I did in fact talk about politics, just close your eyes and count backwards from one hundred to negative fifty, and then open your eyes and you should have forgotten everything you read. If not, tough.

A popular website, zug.com, decided to prank our United States Senators by sending every one of them a letter from a supposed ten-year-old boy whose goal in life was to become a comedian.

The non-existent ten-year-old simply asked for the Senators to respond with their favorite joke. The premise was that he wanted to become a comedian when grew up. Although it was kind of neat to get a response from the Senators, it wasn't the funniest prank in the world. What I did find funny was the wordy responses some of the Senators felt it necessary to send a ten-year-old kid. Take New Jersey Senator Jon S. Corzine, for example:

Dear John:

Thank you for contacting me as a part of your Social Studies project. I apologize for not responding sooner, but the United States Senate mail delivery system has been substantially delayed due to the remediation process each piece of mail must undergo. However, I appreciate the opportunity to be involved with such a unique project.

As you are not a resident of the great State of New Jersey, I thought it would be nice to take this opportunity to share a few fun and interesting facts with you about the State that I call home. New Jersey has a number of State symbols like the violet, our State flower. But did you know that New Jersey has an official dinosaur, too? The Hadrosaurus foulkii dinosaur was first discovered in Haddonfield, New Jersey. The Hadrosaurus was about two-stories tall, over 30 feet long, and an herbivore. Other State symbols include the State insect, the honeybee; the State dance, the square dance; the State animal, the horse; and the state shell, the knobbled whelk or conch shell.

As you may know, New Jersey's nickname is "The Garden State." Back in 1954, when the New Jersey State Legislature considered whether or not to place this slogan on state license plates, a great controversy arose. No one knew why New Jersey was called "The Garden State!" The governor at the time, Governor Meyner, called for an investigation into the

Man, what a mouthful. I'll have to admit that some of the info he gave about New Jersey was kinda neat to me (the square dance is the official dance of New Jersey?), but I'm a nerd and I'm twenty-eight years old. If John were really a ten-year-old kid, he would have probably just scanned down the page looking for the joke, thinking, "I don't remember asking for a history lesson, Bub." The kid said he wanted to be a comedian, not a welcome center tour guide. And what was the deal with that last info paragraph? Over a hundred words talking about origin of "The Garden State" and basically the conclusion was, "we still don't know where it came from, but we sure got a lot of trees and stuff." I did kinda like the joke though.

In case you were wondering what our buddy Hillary Clinton submitted as her joke, don't bother, she didn't reply.

The Gillete M3 Power Razor

I just saw an ad for the Gillette M3 Power razor. It's considered an "advance in shaving."

I'm sure they've tested the thing and it's safe, but something about putting a battery in the handle of a razor and making it vibrate just doesn't sit well with me.

The concept reminds of the old "Lectra Blades" of the Eighties (only took them 20 years or so to come out with the exact same "advance" that Norellco did). My mom had one of those. It scared me. Tie a machette to the side of an air compressor and turn it on next to a cow and see if the cow doesn't freak out.

146

Supposedly, when you turn the thing on, its vibrations cause the hairs to rise, thus resulting in a closer shave.

Other innovations include: 3 "powerglide" blades, which are supposedly an improvement over the Mach3 Turbo's Anti-friction blades, which were supposedly an improvement over the original Mach3 triple-blades; 10, count 'em, 10 microfins, on par with the Mach3 Turbo, as opposed to the modest 5 microfins of the original Mach3 (microfins supposedly help to push the skin down to expose more of the hair, which in turn results in a closer shave—yep, pretty much like the vibrating thing is supposed to do); an indicator strip with even MORE lubrication than the original Mach3; and a redesigned ergonomic handle, since ergonomics have changed over the years.

Wow. All that, and it only costs $15? And I get one replacement blade and am able to shave myself like 4-5 times for that $15? Amazing. As Eddie Murphy would say, "What a bargain; that is the bargain for me."

Future 4 packs of blades cost a modest $12 or so, roughly placing your shaving budget at a reserved $150-ish a year, and that's assuming you're not a Robin Williams-esque-wooly-mammoth-man. I could go to a barber every day and get a hot towel shave for around the same price. Plus I wouldn't have to worry about errantly cutting my head off due to all the vibrations (unless it's an old man that shakes a lot). Heck, I could probably buy a monkey and train him to shave me for that price.

I'm not saying the original Mach3 and even the Mach3 Turbo are bad razors; I actually own one of the original Mach3 razors (2 actually, since I lost the first one for a month or so), and it did indeed provide a great shave. But after paying for a few months of razor blade refills, along with realizing I could get just about as good of a shave out of a good medium-grade disposable or an electric, I stopped burning that hole in my wallet.

But Gillette and their competition will always release new razors as long as someone is willing to pony up the cash. So I'm going to beat them to the punch and make my own super-razor...I'll call it the Uber-Blade 3000.

The Uber-Blade 3000 features a newly designed ergonomic handle that chemically fuses to your hand as soon as you grab it.

The device will feature the now-standard 10 microfins, which we will call micro-hair-pusher-upper-thingies due to copyright law, but the Uber-Blade 3000's are special because hidden between each one there will be specially trained bacteria that are trained to jump out and scare the hairs, which will result in them standing up even further.

The standard lubricating strip will be replaced by a live slug, for all-natural lubrication, which everyone knows is better for your skin, and is overall superior in every way. You will of course, get 2 replacement slugs so that you can get the standard 4-ish shaves before having to buy new blades/slugs. You also get a convenient bowl of margarita salt to dispose of your used slugs.

There will be ten blades on the razor, all made up of four smaller blades, and each coated with a non-friction-anti-snag-no-corrosion-chocolate-flavored treatment and doused with Johnson's No Tears Tangle-removing shampoo just for good measure.

And finally, the best part is the nuclear-powered paint can shaker that it's all attached to for the most intense vibrating hair-raising action ever!

This "advancement in shaving" will be available for whatever your net worth is divided by two. Additional blades/slugs will be approximately the same price.

Tips For Your Visit to Japan

When my friend Alan Nethery visited Japan on a business trip, I felt it necessary to email him these tips that I had learned from living in Japan for three years:

1.)   Try the Coca-cola flavored candy; it's the bomb diggity.

2.)   Laugh a lot for no apparent reason at the end of your sentences; it will help you fit in.

3.)   Don't mention World War 2, especially when applying tip #2

4.)   Try the coffee flavored popsicles; they too are the bomb diggity

5.)   Stock up on toys while you're there; you'll make a fortune on ebay

6.)   Flipping the bird still doesn't mean "You're number 1!" even in Japan

7.)   Go find a Japanese arcade; you'll be amazed

8.)   Try the little round purple grape flavored bubble gum; once again, bomb diggity

9.)   Take as many pictures of improperly translated English signs as possible (see www.engrish.com for examples)

10.) Avoid foods that contain the words "surprise" or "delight," as you will most likely later get a surprise that is not a delight

These are all supposedly true, but if not, just pretend they are and say, "oh, I did not know that. That is very interesting."

- On a Canadian two-dollar bill, the flag flying over the Parliament Building is an American flag
- The youngest Pope ever was eleven years old
- The phrase "rule of thumb" derived from an old English law that stated you couldn't beat your wife with anything wider than your thumb
- Shakespeare invented the words "assassination" and "bump," as well as several names including Jessica, which is many times credited as a Jewish name since the character he assigned it to was a "Jewess"
- The name Wendy was made up for the book "Peter Pan"
- The sentence "the quick brown fox jumps over the lazy dog" uses every letter in the English language
- The longest one-syllable word in the English language is "screeched"
- A rhino's horn is made of a compacted hair-like material

- Elvis had a twin brother named Garon who died at birth. That's why his middle name is Aron; in honor of his brother
- A snail can sleep for three years
- The electric chair was invented by a dentist
- The odds of dying by way of a poisonous spider bite are lower than the odds of dying by way of a champagne cork
- Cat urine will glow under a black light
- The shortest complete sentence in the English language: "I am."

You Can't Find Everything on the Internet

While Hurricane Ivan was blowing through Alabama those of us in Eastern Mississippi got some of the residual winds and rain.

While I was walking to my workplace I saw a huge pinecone get blown off a tree and thump loudly on the ground next to me. My immediate thought was "wow, that would've hurt like the dickens if it hit me on my head." It fell from the top of the tree, which had to be at least fifty feet tall. Then I realized that getting hit in the head by a falling pinecone is something that I've never stopped to ponder. I've never

152

heard of anyone getting popped in the head by one and I've never listed pinecones on my list of threats to my health.

Naturally, I decided to search the internet to see if there were any stories about people getting smacked in the head by a pinecone. Oddly enough, I couldn't find anything. I found a couple of references to people throwing pinecones at people and hitting them, one of someone getting hit in the foot, and one of a wolf in a fictional story getting hit in the nose by one. No references to getting knocked in the head by a naturally falling pinecone. Had I stumped Google?

I thought you could find anything on the internet. Surely someone, somewhere, had been hit on the head by a pinecone. But alas, I found nothing of the sort.

So then it occurred to me, are there other topics that have been totally overlooked by the internet? I did some research and the results were astounding. I could find no information (via Google) on the following topics:

    - Bald-headed fish
    -Seven-foot-tall Fat Red-headed Taiwanese Guy
    - Trampoline Juice
    - Dinosaur Flavoring
    - Good morals are on the rise in America

Almost equally as interesting (and in some cases scary) are some of the subjects I *did* find information on:

- *Unicycles for Midgets*
- *Paris Hilton is smart*
- *Sea Monkey Disease*
- *Michael Jackson is my hero*
- *Morals aren't important*

Now, when I say I found no information on that first set of subjects, I mean any actual information dealing with that exact subject, not if Google came up with any hits or not.

All search engines tend to come up with some sort of hit, regardless of what you type in the search bar. I actually clicked on the links to determine if my topic of choice was actually referred to on the page.

Google is actually pretty hard to stump and get absolutely no results. It's also equally as hard to get only one or two results—probably harder.

Some bored guy fella actually came out with a game called googlewhacking, in which you attempt to find a two-word phrase that when entered into Google only returns a single result. Two or more results do not count, and the words you use have to be real words, as determined by the website www.dictionary.com. If you manage to get a successful googlewhack, you can go to the official googlewhack website, www.googlewhacking.com, and record your whack on the "whack stack."

I've tried it and it's pretty hard. I've managed to get three googlewhacks and that took way longer than I would care to admit. Nonetheless, if you're really, really, really bored you can give googlewhacking a try.

The Greatest Poem Ever Written

Finally, I'd like to present to you a poem I wrote in my early high school years (I think I was a freshman).

I was never a poet, nor a fan of poetry by any stretch of the imagination, but due to the idea of having to do the assignment that a teacher gives you in order to avoid a failing grade prompted me to write this poem.

The result was something so beautiful and so moving that I vowed that if I would ever write a book this poem would be included in it. Yes, Mrs. Gilmer, this one is for you…

Dead Dog

Dead Dog, Dead Dog,
Lying on the road,
Dead Dog, Dead Dog,
Too bad that car made you explode.

Try your best not to weep at the sheer power of that poem.

Outtroduction

I guess that's about all for now—I can check off another box on my "things to do before I die" list.

I still have a lot left on the list, so don't worry about me running out of things to do anytime soon. Included on the list is writing what I would call a "real book," one that involves an actual story, complete with plot and characters.

I'm pretty sure my writing skills aren't up to the task of writing a "real book" yet, but there's always the option of a co-writer. Of course, you never know, there might be a few of you out there that want a Drunken Hamster Electric Boogaloo part Deux. Who knows what the future holds?

Some other things on my "things to do before I die" list:

- Eat one of those huge steaks at one of those restaurants where everyone in your party eats free if you can finish the steak
- Get Zackatony and cheese officially added to a restaurant's menu

- Call Dave Ramsey and yell "I'm Debt Free!!!!!" live on his radio show, then say, "nah, just kidding, credit RULES!" right after he congratulates me
- Develop the ultimate Barbeque Sauce
- Actually beat a new video game without using cheat codes
- Ride a bull for 8 seconds
- Write an entire song without using any goofy lyrics
- Discover the recipe for the special sauce used at the Mexican Kitchen in Columbus, MS
- Get a street named after me
- Finally finish the next installment of the Excalibur 2000 series
- Buy a small island nation and rename it "Baldyland"

Keep in mind that an island is defined by being a mass of land surround on all sides by water. Surely I can find a small one for sale somewhere.

Thanks again for all the support I've gotten from the Tony Marshall Fan Club and all my friends and family that actually knew I was writing this book. I hope you enjoyed it as much as I enjoyed writing it.

I also pray the Lord Jesus Christ comes
into your life and blesses each of you
abundantly.

-- T

*"Then Peter said unto them, Repent,
and be baptized every one of you in the
name of Jesus Christ for the remission
of sins, and ye shall receive the gift of
the Holy Ghost." -- Acts 2:38 KJV*